The
CREATION
CONTROVERSY
The
& SCIENCE
CLASSROOM

Art and Design
Linda Olliver, Director
NSTA Web
Tim Weber, Webmaster
Outreach
Michael Byrnes, Editor-at-Large
Periodicals Publishing
Shelley Carey, Director
Printing and Production
Catherine Lorrain-Hale, Director
Publications Operations
Erin Miller, Manager
sciLINKS
Tyson Brown, Manager

National Science Teachers Association
Gerald F. Wheeler, Excutive Director
David Beacom, Publisher

NSTA Press, NSTA Journals, and the NSTA Web site deliver high-quality resources for science educators.

Shirley Watt Ireton, Director
Judy Cusick, Associate Editor
Carol Duval, Associate Editor
Linda Olliver, Cover Design

The Creation Controvery & The Science Classroom
NSTA stock number: PB069X2
ISBN: 0-87355-184-2
Library of Congress Control Number: 00-132230
Printed in the USA by Kirby Lithographic Company, Inc.
Printed on recycled paper.

An earlier edition of "Modern Science and the Book of Genesis" by James W. Skehan S.J., was published under the same title, ©1986 by the National Science Teachers Association.

The CREATION CONTROVERSY

& *The* SCIENCE CLASSROOM

Modern Science and the Book of Genesis

James W. Skehan S.J., Ph.D.

Director and Professor Emeritus
Weston Observatory, Department of Geology and Geophysics
Boston College

Effective Strategies for Teaching Controversial Topics

Craig E. Nelson, Ph.D.

Professor, Department of Biology
Indiana University

NSTApress
NATIONAL SCIENCE TEACHERS ASSOCIATION
ARLINGTON, VIRGINIA

Contents

An NSTA Position Statement: The Teaching of Evolution

About the Contributors

James W. Skehan S.J., Director and Professor Emeritus, Weston Observatory, Department of Geology and Geophysics, Boston College, received a Ph.D. in Geology from Harvard University, 1953; S.T.B., Bachelor of Sacred Theology; M. Div., Master of Divinity; and S.T.L., Licentiate in Sacred Theology, Weston Jesuit School of Theology, 1954 and 1955. He has been active in research on geological correlations on the North American, European, and African margins of the Atlantic Ocean, and on assembly and dispersal of supercontinents. He is a past president of the International Division of the Geological Society of America.

Craig E. Nelson, Professor of Biology at Indiana University, received a Ph.D. in Zoology from University of Texas in 1966. He has worked extensively with high school biology teachers, especially as co-director of the NSF-sponsored Evolution and Nature of Science Institutes for in-service high school biology teachers (1989–95). He also offers a graduate course, "Alternative Approaches to Teaching College Biology," and has received awards for distinguished teaching from Indiana University, Vanderbilt University, and Northwestern University. His biological research has addressed several questions in evolution and evolutionary ecology.

Gerald Skoog is a past president of the National Science Teachers Association and Helen DeVitt Jones Professor, Curriculum and Instruction, College of Education at Texas Tech University. Skoog, author of numerous science textbooks, chaired the committee to draft NSTA's current position paper on the teaching of evolution, and in January 2000 was selected to the Texas Science Hall of Fame.

Acknowledgements

Dr. Skehan: I acknowledge Gerald Skoog, past president of the National Science Teachers Association, who, during his service as -resident (1985–86), recognized the potential for mischief that the creation science movement represented in the lives of teachers of science. Although unforeseen at the time, the original edition of "Modern Science and the Book of Genesis" was also a fringe benefit for many teachers of religion who had little background in science.

In particular I acknowledge the continued encouragement that I have received from Albert W. Bally, Henry Carothers Wiess Emeritus Professor, Department of Geology and Geophysics of Rice University, to answer "scientific creationists" who have succeeded in holding up the teaching of some major advances in geological science. Professor Bally, past president of the Geological Society of America, wrote the introduction to the 1986 edition. I am also very grateful to Frederick L. Moriarty S.J., Professor Emeritus, Weston Jesuit School of Theology, and Department of Theology, Boston College, for reviewing this manuscript as well as the 1986 edition. I wish to acknowledge Erin Miller of the NSTA staff for her generous and congenial assistance during the production of the present book.

Dr. Nelson: My deepest debt is to my students who have been willing to tell me what they understood, what they didn't, and where they were puzzled or bothered. I also have received immense help in thinking about these issues from Martin Nickels and Jean Beard, who co-directed the Evolution and Nature of Science Institutes with me, and from the many high school teachers who participated in those institutes. Extensive comments on the manuscript from John Labov of the National Research Council, several anonymous reviewers, Erin Miller at NSTA, and several of my colleagues at Indiana University (especially comments from Nancy Beecher and Eric Osnas) led to substantial improvements. Any remaining lapses and misjudgments are, of course, mine.

NSTA would like to thank the many people who contributed to the development of this book, including Gerald Skoog, John R. Staver, John Labov, Jeffrey D. Weld, Brad Williamson, Mary Liston Liepold, Lawrence Bellipanni, Margaret McIntyre, Mary Beavis, Dorothy Gabel, Frederick L. Moriarity S.J., Charles L. Drake, Preston Cloud, and William D. Sullivan S.J. *The Creation Controversy & The Science Classroom* is produced by NSTA Press: Shirley Watt Ireton, director; Beth Daniels, managing editor; Erin Miller, associate editor; Carol Duval, associate editor; Jessica Green, assistant editor; Anne Early, editorial assistant. Erin Miller is the project editor for *The Creation Controversy & The Science Classroom*. Copyediting by Cara Young; cover design by Linda Olliver.

Foreword

In using science to explain natural events, Copernicus, Galileo, and Darwin opened some doors that led many of their contemporaries to view the world in a different manner. Today, scientists open these doors at a faster pace, and the new knowledge that emerges often challenges traditional thought and poses ethical questions. For a variety of reasons, citizens may challenge the process and products of science in an uninformed manner. Because of the multifaceted consequences of the wrongful use of the conclusions and products of science, it is important that citizens have a voice in determining how science is used. However, this voice should be informed.

Despite its centrality to understanding the natural world and much of today's research, evolution's rightful place in the science curriculum has not been attained because of the persistent opposition of antievolutionists and their enablers. The opposition and enablement have been fueled by a lack of understanding of the methods of science and, too often, by an uninformed view of the purpose and context of Genesis and how it was written. Dr. Skehan, in this revision of his earlier important work, skillfully clarifies the differences in the basis of the claims of religion and science. In detailing the history and theological meaning of the book of Genesis, Skehan shows why Genesis is not the literal explanation for the nature and history of the natural world.

Students who repeatedly experience the strategies described by Dr. Nelson in this volume should gain a solid understanding of the nature of science. They will learn how to test claims and ideas in an informed manner, regardless of their origin. They will learn how to consider alternatives to various claims and the benefits and consequences of accepting or rejecting them. Also, Nelson shows the differences in how basic science and creationism answer important questions about the origin and evolution of the universe and life.

I am confident that this small volume will provide readers with additional understanding of the nature of science and the relationship between science and religion. Hopefully, this understanding and the use of the strategies will facilitate the professional practice of science teachers. These teachers have the immense task of preparing students for life and work in a century where advances in our understanding of the natural world continue to open doors that will challenge long-held views and pose difficult ethical questions.

Gerald Skoog
Helen DeVitt Jones Professor of Education
Texas Tech University
NSTA President, 1985–86

Modern Science
and
the Book of Genesis

James W. Skehan, S.J.

Many religious people, including scientists, hold that God created the universe and the various processes driving physical and biological evolution and that these processes then resulted in the creation of galaxies, our solar system, and life on Earth. This belief, sometimes termed *theistic evolution,* is not in disagreement with scientific explanations of evolution. Indeed, it reflects the remarkable and inspiring character of the physical universe revealed by cosmology, paleontology, molecular biology, and many other scientific disciplines.

The advocates of "creation science," a proactive kind of Christian religion that purports to be scientific, hold a variety of viewpoints about the age of Earth. Some creationists claim that Earth and the universe are relatively young, perhaps only 6,000 to 10,000 years old. Some creationists believe that the present physical form of Earth can be explained by "catastrophism," with a worldwide flood as one of the catastrophes, and that all living things (including humans) were created miraculously, essentially in the forms we see them today.

Other advocates of creation science are willing to accept that Earth, the planets, and the stars may have existed for millions of years. But they argue that the various types of organisms, and especially humans, could only have come about through supernatural intervention, because they show "intelligent design."

There are no valid scientific data or calculations to substantiate the belief that Earth was created just a few thousand years ago. Independent scientific methods consistently give an age for Earth and the solar system of about five billion years, and an age for our galaxy and the universe that is two to three times greater. The conclusions derived from these methods make the origin of the universe as a whole intelligible, lend coherence to many different branches of science, and form the core of a remarkable body of knowledge about the origins and behavior of the physical world.[1]

Creationism and Teachers

Creationism is a problem for teachers partly because a number of state and local school boards have taken an anti-evolution stance. The National Academy of Sciences,[2] the National Science Teachers Association, and many other respected organizations have published responses to this misguided political activity.

Vocal and influential proponents of "creation science" are disseminating scientific misinformation.[3] They compound the problem by mingling defective science with a fundamentalist reading of the first five books of the Hebrew Bible, the Pentateuch or Torah, to support a young Earth interpretation. Creationists establish a false dichotomy, denying that there can be any accommodation between creation and evolution for believing scientists.

Teachers of science must be prepared to deal with scientific and religious questions concerning the origins of the universe, of Earth, and of life. The old-style (young Earth) creation science claims that the creation stories in the book of Genesis should be understood literally in both their religious elements and their primitive world view, and they adopt the position that both should be taught in the public schools as modern science. A number of proponents of "intelligent-design" and "theistic-science" have emerged in the creation debate. One dominant new-style creationist position appears to misunderstand the nature of relevant scientific issues, and although the fundamentalist premises are vaguely stated, appears to be an outgrowth of the old-style creation science. Other proponents of "intelligent design" clearly are at pains to distance themselves from the young Earth and anti-evolution position of the old-style creation science.[4]

Both scientific education and religious education are important in a civilized society. Today's teachers must be able to make a clear distinction between science and religion in a manner that does justice to both. Teachers must be able to help students from varied backgrounds, first to recognize the difference between scientific and religious language and approaches, and second, to realize that there is no necessary conflict between interpretations of data from scientific studies and religious beliefs based on the Bible. Scientific discourse is fundamentally different from religious discourse, as I will attempt to make clear.

Today many sincere young people face the same apparent conflict that I faced as a high school and university student in the 1940s. At that time we Catholics were encouraged to interpret Genesis in a rather fundamentalist way because Church leaders feared that we might be led astray by discussions of evolution. Thanks to a number of excellent teachers, I learned to rely on scientific methods to explain how Earth originated and evolved, as well as how human life and other life forms originated. I also learned that the creation story presented in Genesis describes the initial origin of the universe and that, once in existence, the universe evolved and became the proper object for scientific study. I learned about the divine and human authorship of the Bible, both its historically conditioned character and its divine inspiration.

The reconciliation of faith and reason delivers the student from a state of confusion about important areas of life portrayed as contradictions by some fundamentalists. Instead of having to choose between science and religion, between the book of God's revelation and the "book of nature," as our ancestors called the natural world, the student can appreciate and learn from both, or at least understand the position of those who accept both.

Religious Science? Scientific Religion?

Science and religion are very different from each other. Although most people seem to understand this fact, many have difficulty explaining how they differ. Creation science is an oxymoron because it involves contradictory claims. Religion cannot be both religion and science.

Religion is concerned with God. Langdon Gilkey, Professor Emeritus in the Divinity School of the University of Chicago, made this clear in *Creationism on Trial: Evolution and God at Little Rock*: "Religious discourse in western religions refers to God, a transcendent being, one who is the source and ground of creaturely beings, and, therefore, not part of the creaturely system." Gilkey continues:

> Discourse about God, such as 'God intended such a result,' or 'God's intent is shown by his design of the universe,' is language that refers to a personal and purposive God, language that makes use of symbols or analogy. Creation is a religious term, which indicates that God is the subject responsible for the universe coming into existence. Because God is referred to as the origin of the system of nature, he cannot be part of nature. Science is concerned with the study of some aspect of nature.[5]

In *McLean v. Arkansas*, a 1981 court case that overturned a state law mandating the teaching of creation science *as science* in the public school system, Gilkey clearly explained why the act of creation cannot be part of science:

> Creation is a divine act....In our religious tradition—in both Scripture and creed—the first important thing said about God: God creates. It is the first foundation of Jewish and Christian religion ... [T]he divine act of creation cannot be a part of science, for science inquires only within the system of nature and cannot go beyond it, as religion, monotheistic religion, essentially does. Unlike scientific investigation, creation as a religious symbol does not reveal matters of factual information, but does reveal that, in whatever way it may have originated, the universe is of God, and has meaning and purpose...
>
> Religion cannot provide us with answers as to when the universe arose, or the processes by which the universe has changed through time. These are scientific questions. Scientific discourse, by contrast, can speak only about creaturely objects, that is those that have come into being in time, and which are, therefore, not transcendent.[6]

Because science is concerned with the study of non-transcendent parts of the universe, science became possible only after the creation of the universe had taken place. So-called creation science misinterprets science and scientific methods as well as theology and theological methods. It interprets the Genesis stories as telling us *how* and *when* creation took place, rather than telling us *why* God created the universe or *what* that statement means. When we say that science excludes God *methodologically*, we mean only that the methods of science are in and of themselves incapable of discovering God as the author of the universe. We are saying that scientific investigation is limited in a way analogous to, but different from, the way in which science is limited. This does not mean that scientists as human beings are incapable of finding God by faith; it means merely that the methods of science are limited to discovering information of a scientific character. On the other hand, religion cannot reveal the age of Earth and the universe or other items of factual information.

How Knowledge Has Evolved Through Time

Throughout the ages both Christians and Jews have looked to the Bible first and foremost as a guide and support for their religious lives. Some, going further, wanted to find out the age of Earth and the universe. Lacking modern scientific tools and current biblical perspectives, they looked to the book of Genesis, which tells the story of God creating the world and Adam and Eve. Accordingly, many respected early biblical scholars turned to Genesis to calculate the antiquity of Earth and of humankind. Before science began to produce reliable data about the age and history of Earth, its life forms, and other aspects of the natural history of the universe, reasonable people used the sources of information they had available.

Over the past 150 years, however, advances in scientific research have brought to light evidence that Earth is nearly five billion years old and the universe is considerably older at about 12 billion years. During the first billion years of its formation, Earth was evolving physically and chemically. The earliest life forms yet discovered are about 3,500 million years old, and the record in the rocks tells us that the human genus *Homo* evolved sometime between 2.5 and 2 million years ago.[7]

As a result of these advances in scientific knowledge, the evolution of life forms is widely accepted as a reasonable explanation for the progressively more complex fossils preserved through geological time in the rocks, and as an explanation for the diversity of modern organisms. As ideas concerning evolution have developed from the study of geology and biology, those who believe in the Bible as the word of God have taken up positions along a spectrum of beliefs.

At one end are the creation science proponents, who maintain a literal interpretation of the Genesis creation narrative despite the evidence from science and other fields of study. These individuals interpret the results of scholarly research as diametrically opposed to their religious beliefs, and maintain that no reconciliation is possible between belief in the Bible and belief in theories of biological evolution. On the other end are those in mainstream Christianity and mainstream Judaism who find no conflict between biblical teachings and scientific theories regarding evolution and the great age of Earth. In between are a significant number of fundamentalists and evangelicals who hold a modified literal interpretation of Genesis and accept the standard geological data on the age of Earth.

Fundamentalism and Fundamentalist Religion

The term *fundamentalism* is used in at least two related but clearly distinguishable senses. It may designate a conservative type of Christian thought that became influential in the second half of the nineteenth and first half of the twentieth centuries. Some of the people to whom this name is applied today, such as creation science proponents, perceive it as a hostile term implying narrowness or bigotry.

Fundamentalism is also the name of a specific conservative movement begun in the United States in 1909, devoted to propagating a definite program of five points of doctrine set forth as fundamental. Its pivotal point is the literal inerrancy and infallibility of the Bible. One of the most famous fundamentalists of this type was William Jennings Bryan, who won *Tennessee v. John Scopes*, a 1925 court case against a public high school teacher charged with teaching evolution.

It is generally conceded, however, that the effect of the Scopes "Monkey Trial" was to discredit fundamentalism in the public mind. Thus, with time, the overt conflict between fundamentalism and science decreased, and the central body of conservative evangelical thought came to accept the validity of evolution—the major focus of the earlier controversy. Many "fundamentalists" today, especially those who accept the results of science, prefer to be called "conservative evangelicals." This is not the group promoting creation science.

Evangelical Christians hold a wide range of beliefs that relate the interpretation of Genesis to the findings of modern science. Of these, only "fiat creationism," which adopts the Ussher-Lightfoot chronology described later, rejects evolution entirely. Fiat creationism, the most rigid of evangelical theories, is the specific, programmatic fundamentalism upheld by Henry Morris, Duane Gish, and their followers who have played leadership roles in the creation science movement. They scathingly denounce the more liberal positions that other fundamentalists have developed, including the Gap Theory, which suggests that billions of years may have occurred between events described in Genesis 1:1 and Genesis 1:2, and the Day-Age Theory, which interprets the biblical days of creation as geological epochs. Moreover, fiat creationists object to efforts by liberal fundamentalists to harmonize the Biblical chronology with geological time because they believe that such accommodation is inevitably followed by acceptance of the evolutionary system.

Creation science has long been unalterably opposed to biological evolution, especially macroevolution. Henry Morris, as Director of the Institute for Creation Research, explained one reason for this position: "The theory of evolution has dominated our society, especially the schools, for almost a hundred years, and its influence is largely responsible for our present-day social, political, and moral problems."[8]

Creation science proponents regard Genesis as the *total* explanation of the origin of all things.[9] Theistic evolutionists, on the other hand, among whom I number myself, regard Genesis as a religious document composed by inspired authors to present a religious message. Its primitive worldview, or cosmology, is the story line that carries the central religious message, but is not itself the message. Theistic evolutionists, in summary, grant to science its proper role of unraveling the history of the evolution of the universe, Earth, living beings, and other creatures, and understand that its established theories do not, and should not, threaten sound religious beliefs.

What the Bible Teaches

Mainstream biblical scholars focus on the intentions of the authors of Genesis and the other four books that comprise the first section of the Bible. These books were written by deeply religious authors who saw history not merely as events that happened to people, but as the record of God's dealings with a special people. Genesis was written to tell the Jews who they were, how and why they were chosen as God's people, what marvelous things God had done for them, and what God expected of them. It was not composed as history for its own sake, but as history whose purpose was to communicate religious truth.

St. Augustine recognized in roughly 400 A.D. that the literal interpretation of the Genesis story of creation taking place over six days involved a theological misunderstanding. He realized that "if at creation God was bringing time and space into being, the act of creation *of* time could not be *in* time and *of* space could not be *in* space." Thus he reasoned that the divine creative act must transcend time—that is, be at a "moment" that "precedes" every moment—for it is the act in which all moments come into being."[10] St. Augustine reasoned that creation *ex nihilo,* or out of nothing, by a transcendent God was the supernatural act that brought both time and space instantaneously into being along with the universe. After that moment natural processes would be at work.

Early biblical commentators recognized, as we do, that Genesis 1–11 is an imaginative narrative that uses poetic language and contains much imagery and many figures of speech. Still, lacking scientific methods capable of resolving questions about the age of Earth, these commentators followed a reasonable course of interpretation for their times in accepting its chronology at face value.

The Genesis of Genesis

Over the past century reliable information that was not available to earlier scholars became accessible from scientific studies. This knowledge conflicted with interpretations of time intervals calculated from Scripture.

In earlier centuries the Bible was commonly accepted as God's word in the narrow sense, as though God had dictated every word. If Moses was the author of

Genesis, and if its first chapters describe events that nobody but God could have seen, then, it was concluded, God must have revealed Genesis just as we have it. Today we have more information available to us about how the Bible itself came into being than did our predecessors. Modern biblical scholarship maintains that Genesis was written under divine inspiration, but the human writers assembled their materials and carried out their work in the same way that writers have throughout the ages. Today we have direct evidence to show that the authors of Genesis derived their materials from written and oral sources that were readily at hand, such as the Babylonian creation myth and the Mesopotamian story of a "worldwide" flood.

Chapters 1–11 of Genesis use fragments of myth, legend, and folklore, whereas the patriarchal stories in chapters 12–50 are reminiscent of family sagas. Israel's historians made use of materials of all kinds, often modified from those of their pagan neighbors or captors. These include ancient creation stories, genealogical lists, songs, proverbs, legends, records of customs, institutions, and idioms. All contributed to the authors' purposes and were refashioned accordingly.

External Evidence

In many cases the biblical authors used a traditional source. Unfortunately, these writers did not usually inform us when they were using or adapting parallel writings, as was done in Genesis 1:1–2:4a, the creation narrative. By comparing the Genesis text with the Babylonian creation myth Enuma Elish ("When on High"), we can see parallels as well as pronounced differences.

Archaeological discoveries of tablets recording the Babylonian creation story have shed light on that story and its relation to Genesis. Enuma Elish is an epic poem of approximately a thousand lines recorded on seven clay tablets. The first fragments were discovered by Austen H. Layard, Hormuzd Rassam, and George Smith during expeditions between the years 1848 and 1876 among the ruins of the great library of King Ashurbanipal (c. 668–630 B.C.) at Niniveh. Subsequent explorations through 1929 led to the discovery of all the remaining tablets except for a large portion of Tablet V.

George Smith of the British Museum, the first to publish an account of the epic, translated and discussed all of the pieces identified prior to 1876. The resemblance of their contents to the initial chapters of the Bible immediately appealed to a very wide circle of students. Since then, this story has been copied and translated by many Assyriologists, especially as new, related tablets have been found.[11]

The left column of the table on the next page outlines the story of the origin of the gods as presented in the Enuma Elish.[12] Marduk was the creator of Earth in this account. The authors of Genesis offered a new theology of creation, with the one God of Israel being the Creator. The well-known topics and sequence of Genesis are presented in the right-hand column. The authors of Genesis borrowed many of the topics of the older Babylonian story, but rejected those which involved a contrary theological perspective.

In the language of drama, we might say that the props are the same in these two creation narratives, but the characters are very different. The authors of Genesis present a primitive cosmology of their time to teach the origin of all things in God, emphasizing God's power as transcendent Supreme Being. Whereas the earlier Babylonian creation epic, which is generally dated from at least 2000 B.C., depicted creation as the result of a struggle between the gods and the forces of chaos, the biblical account stresses the effortless activity of the one God. The imagery borrowed from Enuma Elish and other accounts serves the authors' polemic against the error of polytheism, the idea that there are many gods. The table below highlights the similarities of sequence, as well as the contrasts in religious points of view.

Internal Evidence

We may discover what kind of document Genesis is from a study of the text itself. Some stories, such as the creation narrative of Chapters 1 and 2, consist of two parallel accounts woven together by the biblical authors. Differences between these accounts in style, in detail, and even in the name for God permit us to distinguish

ENUMA ELISH	GENESIS
An account of the birth of the gods and various conflicts between them	
Divine spirit and cosmic matter are coexistent and coeternal	Divine word creates cosmic matter and exists independently of it
Primeval chaos; Ti'amat, enveloped in darkness	The Earth is a desolate waste, with darkness covering the deep (tehom)
Light emanating from the gods	The creation of light and the separation of light and darkness
Marduk's work of creation (a) The creation of the firmament	The creation of the firmament and the dividing of the waters
(b) The creation of dry land	The creation of dry land, the sea, and plant life
(c) The creation of the luminaries	The creation of the luminaries, the creatures of the sea, and the birds
(d) The creation of humans; the building and dedication of Esagila, the temple complex	The creation of land animals and humans; God instructs Adam and Eve and blesses them
The gods rest and celebrate; the hymn to the creator, Marduk	God rests from all his work and sanctifies the seventh day
Epilogue	

component parts. Evidence derived from literary analysis of the Bible has led most non-literalist scripture scholars of the past 200 years to interpret Genesis as a composite of several documents, or traditions, as they are called.[13] This interpretation of the composite nature of Genesis and of the other four books of the Pentateuch is referred to as the *documentary hypothesis*. Hypotheses, by their very nature, are open to modification and, in some cases, rejection. A hypothesis is not a sacred cow. It invites examination and modification by competent scholars, and if it is found to be no longer valid it is dropped.

The most significant traditions in Genesis are referred to as J (Yahwist), E (Elohist), and P (Priestly). Although it is not a tradition as such, we also refer to R, a redactor, or later editor, who refashioned the material belonging to the several traditions into the form in which it has been recorded in the earliest known manuscripts comprising the Hebrew Bible. On the basis of archaeological evidence and the early written records of Near-Eastern peoples, these traditions can probably be traced as far back as the tenth century B.C.

The earliest tradition is called Yahwist, or J (scholars follow the German spelling, Jahweh) because it uses the divine name said to have been first revealed to Moses at the burning bush (Exodus 3). This tradition is generally attributed to a Judean writer of the tenth century B.C., writing during the reign of Solomon (c. 960–920 B.C.). The Yahwist gave Genesis its narrative framework, characterized by a distinctive vocabulary and a vivid, colorful style replete with anthropomorphisms, as when God is described as walking in the Garden of Eden.

The Elohist tradition, E, uses Elohim as its title for God, a name whose root meaning appears to designate power—"the Force," we might say today. It also has a distinctive vocabulary and a somber style, which depicts the relationship of God with humankind as less intimate than it appears in the Yahwist passages. God remains invisible, speaking from the midst of fire or cloud, and frequently speaks in dreams or acts through the agency of angels.

The Priestly tradition, P, having an obvious concern for liturgy, organized and systematized Genesis, beginning in the first chapter and running throughout, so that the narrative has a strong liturgical and legalistic flavor. For example, the creation story in the Priestly tradition is cast in the framework of six working days and one Sabbath day for rest, thus placing great emphasis on the Sabbath as holy. This document as we have it probably dates from the period of the exile of Judah in Babylon (587–538 B.C.), though it incorporates much earlier material as well. The Redactor, or final editor, put Genesis and the other books of the Pentateuch into essentially the form in which they occur in the most ancient Hebrew manuscripts so far known, from about 400 B.C. The ideas stressed by this editor are mainly those of J and P, with some elements of E.[14]

About Documentary Hypothesis

The main point I wish to make in discussing the documentary hypothesis and its many variations is that Genesis in particular, and the Pentateuch in general, have a complex literary history. This could not have been a single composition dictated by God to Moses, as creation science maintains. The documentary hypothesis is offered merely as that, an hypothesis that tries to provide some explanation for the literary complexity of the first five books of the Bible. It plays a lesser role in biblical scholarship today than it did formerly, precisely because it is so generally accepted. The newer "literary criticism"[15] while recognizing the historical usefulness of the documentary hypothesis, focuses on the internal, rhetorical workings of the text. This approach places great emphasis on the details, dramatic tensions, nuances, and sheer power of the text itself.

Despite claims by creationists[16] and conservative biblical scholars that the hypothesis has been disproved, and despite ongoing discussion about methods, it is generally accepted today by the vast majority of those in the mainstream of scriptural studies. On the other hand, the creationist's fundamental assumption is that today's Bible, in an approved English translation, is to be taken literally. This is the only legitimate approach, they claim, because the Bible is a factual narrative that for all practical purposes was dictated word for word by God. Creation science implies that the Bible must not be interpreted by the same techniques that are applied to other literary works.

The Age of Earth as Interpreted from the Bible

One key creationist assumption is that the biblical narrative contains the basis for computing the interval from the creation of Earth to the birth of Jesus Christ, and that this interval plus the date A.D. is the true age of Earth. On this basis creationists hold that Earth may be as young as 6,000 years.[17]

I will merely outline the general method that two venerable Scripture scholars used to arrive at this figure of 6,000 years for Earth's age. James Ussher (1581–1656), Archbishop of Armagh and Vice-Chancellor of Trinity College, Dublin, a biblical scholar, concluded in 1650 that the world was created in 4004 B.C. Well into the twentieth century Ussher's date for creation has been commonly added as a marginal note to the Authorized Version of the English Bible. According to Stephen Jay Gould, it was still being printed in the Gideon Bibles in 1977.[18]

A number of current textbooks join Ussher's calculations with those of his contemporary, John Lightfoot. Lightfoot, who distinguished himself as a biblical scholar and eventually became Vice Chancellor of Cambridge, published his observations eight years before Ussher. He specified the time of the creation of Adam (not of Earth) as early morning at the autumnal equinox of 3928 B.C. Lightfoot arrived at his conclusion by totaling the ages of individuals in the Bible and adding the then-present date 1644, to give a sum of "5,572 years just finished since the Creation, and the year 5,573 of the world's age now newly begun this September at the Equinox."[19]

Tallying up such great intervals of time to produce a chronology was no small task. Ussher compared four different versions of scripture to arrive at the period between the creation and the flood, each yielding a different date. In the course of time, more than 300 such chronologies have been attempted, and nearly all of them arrive at a figure near 6,000 years from the time of creation to the present. Present-day creationists are sometimes willing to accept a figure as high as 10,000 years.

New Data: Evidence from the Earth

While the Reverend Drs. Lightfoot and Ussher were calculating Earth's age from Scripture, others had already begun to look to Earth itself for answers. Six years before Lightfoot's death in 1675, Nicolaus Steno, a medical doctor and specialist in the anatomy of sharks, a deeply religious scientist and later a Catholic priest, established the foundations for the science of stratigraphy. Steno surmised that fossils were the remains of ancient animals, rather than God's practice creations snuffed out by the flood, as some had claimed. The International Geological Congress named Steno the "Father of Modern Geology" about 1876.

In 1785 James Hutton offered the concept of uniformitarianism, which proposed that the physical composition of Earth was the result of gradual geological processes operating over long periods of time and still in operation today. Engineer William Smith made stratigraphic analyses in 1799 that confirmed Steno's hypotheses of 1669. After demonstration by James Hall, and inclusion in Sir Charles Lyell's *Principles of Geology*,[20] the idea began to gain respectability.

Over the course of the nineteenth century, physicists made calculations based on the theories of Galileo, Newton, and others, and proposed estimates ranging from 75,000 to 40 million years for the age of Earth. Lord Kelvin held to the upper end in an address before the 1897 annual meeting of the American Association for the Advancement of Science. Although Kelvin was not yet aware of its implications, Henri Becquerel had just discovered radioactivity in uranium salts in 1896, the same year in which Marie Sklodowska-Curie isolated radium and Wilhelm Roentgen discovered the x-ray. Together, these discoveries would make it possible to measure the length of time since specific rocks were formed.[21]

Ernest Rutherford, in 1905, was the first to suggest that radioactive materials could be used to date rocks. He succeeded in dating a uranium sample in his Montreal laboratory the following year. Bertram Boltwood, discoverer of the first isotope (an isotope of thorium which he called *ionium*), also published the ages of dated minerals in the ensuing years. In 1913 Frederick Soddy refined the process by clarifying the nature of isotopes. Already it was becoming clear from empirical evidence that Earth and its components dated in the billions of years.[22]

Scientists use the amounts of parent isotopes and daughter products present in a rock sample to gauge the time between that rock's crystallization and the present. Measurements based on the known decay rates of uranium, rubidium, potassium, and samarium (assumed to be relatively constant over time) reveal the dates of the formation of the substances in which they occur, and by inference, of any other rocks that are obviously related in age. When we date the crystallization of a once-molten granite, for example, we also know that the surrounding sedimentary rocks, into which the granite was intruded when it crystallized, must be older than the granite itself. We can date sedimentary rocks from the fossils they contain. But if these strata overlie, and thus must be younger than, other radioactively dated rocks, we can establish an absolute age range, if not a precise date of formation, for the sedimentary rocks—even if they themselves contain no datable materials.

Age dating of meteorites has revealed that all but a few are somewhere in the vicinity of 4.4 billion years old, no matter what their composition. The fact that there are few known meteorites of any other age, regardless of when they fell to Earth, suggests strongly that they originated in other bodies of the solar system that formed at the same time as did Earth. If so, then the meteorites also help us to calculate Earth's age.[23]

Lead from Earth falls on the same isochron (a line on a chart connecting points derived from measured isotopic ratios that represent the same age) as the lead in meteorites, and thus indicates an age for both of 4.6+ billion years. We infer from this that both came from the same primordial source, at the same time. Because quantities of uranium 235 and uranium 238 increase as we move backward in time (and uranium decays into lead at a slow but precisely known rate), we may assume that quantities of lead 207 and lead 206 were proportionally smaller than they are now. As we compute the decreasing quantities of lead 207, we conclude that Earth's supply must have been zero at 5.6 billion years ago. On the basis of these two measurements we conclude that Earth must be younger than 5.6 billion years and older than 4.5 billion years.[24]

Geologists studying fossil-bearing sediments have worked out a "clock" that is accurate enough to distinguish the relative ages of rock units as small as a few meters thick, which may represent periods of time of less than a million years. (A million is a large number, of course, but a million years is only about 1/5000th of Earth's history.) The entire geologic record of these sediments has been analyzed and subdivided into a scheme of eons, eras, periods, and absolute ages.

The figure on the next page uses a one-month calendar as a model for the history of Earth. The most eventful divisions have all been collapsed into the last three days. Perhaps the most important time boundaries are those at 544 million years ago,[25] the beginning of the Cambrian period; 245 million years ago, the Permian extinction; and 65 million years ago, the extinction of the dinosaurs and the rise of mammals. The Pliocene deposits, containing the oldest bones thus far assigned to *Homo*, are about 2.4 million years old.[26]

The oldest dated Moon rock is about 4.4 billion years old, and the oldest Earth rock, from Greenland, about 4.1 billion years. The oldest traces of life—bacteria-like structures found in a torrid region of Western Australia whimsically named North Pole—are about 3.5 billion years old. At 544 million years ago, the beginning of Cambrian time, we first notice the appearance of relatively sophisticated organisms, existing in such profusion and variety that we can safely describe the Cambrian seas as teeming with life.[27]

One-Month Calendar of Earth

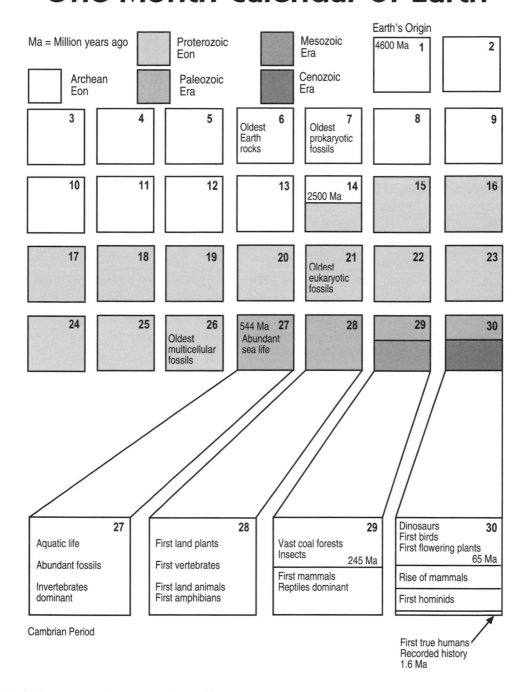

Evidence from the Creatures

It is clear from the fossil record that over time, life forms have changed dramatically but gradually from the simple single-celled organisms of 3.5 billion years ago into animals as complex as humans. About the same time that Steno was learning matter's laws from the rocks, a French naturalist, Georges Buffon, began to notice some interesting things about animals. Comparative anatomy supports the inferences derived from paleontology about descent from a common ancestor. If each animal had been specially created for its own habitat, as was supposed prior to the time of Buffon, it might be expected that the skeletons of each life form would have a unique design.

Erasmus Darwin, grandfather of Charles Darwin, and Buffon's student Jean Baptiste Lamarck were among the nineteenth-century scientists who paved the way for Charles Darwin's *On the Origin of Species* in 1859. But because the discoveries of paleontology and stratigraphy were still almost unknown, Charles Darwin (who called his theory "descent with modification") worried about the scarcity of evidence for the intermediate stages of modification. The fossilized remains of *Archaeopteryx*, a creature partway between reptile and bird, provided the first-found link in 1861. Like every such discovery in the years that followed, the find initiated a search for other forms that would have occupied the spaces before and after *Archaeopteryx*'s existence.

Creationists then and now have seized on Darwin's doubts as ammunition against his theory. But the record is there, for their examination and ours. Although gaps still remain—for your students to fill someday?—the museums of the world contain more than 100 million fossils that have been identified and dated by thousands of paleontologists. From these studies, and those of tens of thousands of other scientists, we can trace a complex and awe-inspiring process.

By the time of the Cambrian "explosion" of life forms at 544 million years ago, representatives of most of the phyla had become equipped with skeletons. Before that time, most organisms had lacked hard parts, such as shells, which form easy-to-recognize fossils. In the absence of easily preserved shell fossils, for example, detailed and accurate geological dating for the Proterozoic and latter part of the Archean eons had to be done on the basis of radiometric age dating of mainly igneous and metamorphic rocks. From the beginning of the Cambrian, the record is relatively easier to read than prior to it.[28]

Trilobites and fish first appeared and became important in the Cambrian period; trees and land plants in the Silurian and Devonian; reptiles in the Late Paleozoic to Triassic and extending through Cretaceous; and small mammals in the Triassic. Humans came on the scene in the Pleistocene epoch—the last 10 minutes of the thirtieth day, in the figure on page 19. The final 30 seconds represent the span of recorded history.[29]

Creationism versus Science

Creationism: The Appeal to Authority

The creation science response to evidence from physics, geology, chemistry, biology, and the related sciences is still the one that biblical literalists were struggling to maintain in the nineteenth century.

I believe that I fairly summarize their position as follows: "If there is any contradiction between a literal interpretation of the Bible and knowledge derived from scientific studies, the latter cannot be true because God's word was dictated verbatim to Moses and therefore cannot be false." A fundamental point in their quarrel with science is the biblically based position that the age of Earth is about 6,000 years old—certainly no older than 10,000 years. Earth and everything on it was created in six days. Adam was created directly by God in his image and likeness; therefore humans can in no way have evolved from lower mammals. In addition, creation science, masquerading as science, rejects well-established methods of seeking scientific truth through research, by which scientists develop hypotheses, theories, and models to explain the data.

These assumptions by creation science are central issues for us because they relate not only to the validity of scientific studies, and especially those in the life, Earth, and astronomical sciences, but also to the understanding of God's word through a sound and reverent application of critical method. The creation science position basically holds that all of the most important truths are explicit in the Bible, and that many conclusions or theories based on the results of scientific studies, such as evolution or the age of the universe and Earth, are illusory.

Sincere people of earlier generations did the best they could with what they knew. Today, however, abundant resources are at hand, so that solidly founded science and religion can not only coexist peacefully, but may mutually enrich the practitioners of each, should they so desire.

Science: The Appeal to Evidence

Although creation science proponents claim not to be opposed to science, it is clear that they reject one of the most important parts of the work that experts in the fields of science do, namely the development of models and theories to explain data. Creation scientists either do not grasp or choose to ignore the nature of theory, claiming that a widely accepted explanation of the data by competent scientists is *only* a theory.

Characteristically, creation science claims that "there is no scientific proof" for evolutionary theory, to which they are unalterably opposed. But no respectable scientist claims that the evidence for a particular theory of evolution is so compelling and complete that it should be regarded as "proven, " meaning "completely understood," including its mechanism. Strictly speaking, a theory cannot be proven in the same sense in which a mathematical theorem can be proven. Theories are erected on evidence. As studies proceed, the evidence increases, the theories are modified, and our understanding improves.

By now experts have presented evidence for evolution that is so massive and convincing that the general validity of the theory is logically demonstrated. From Darwin to the present, the best available data at any given time have provided a basis for modifying specific theories of the evolutionary process. A given theory of evolution in 1880 must be very different from one in 1980 or 2080 because, on the basis of new evidence, our understanding of the theory itself evolves. However, it is in the nature of scientific investigation that the strong corroboration of a theory is secured by evidence. Overwhelming evidence for evolution and uniformitarianism has come from molecular biology, embryology, taxonomy, genetics, zoology, comparative anatomy, physiology, geology, stratigraphy, paleontology, paleoanthropology, physics, chemistry, and astronomy.

The amount and variety of evidence tracing the persistent process of evolution throughout most of Earth's history is so great that geologists generally accept evolution as "proven"—"proof" being a logical deduction as to the cogency of the evidence: a theory so convincing that prudence dictates acceptance.

One of the objectives of scientific investigation is to try to discover mechanisms; however, the demonstration of the logical validity of a theory is independent of the discovery of the mechanism. For example, plate tectonic theory in geology has now been generally accepted among geologists by the accumulation of massive amounts of evidence, although its mechanism is not yet fully understood.

Two Kinds of Knowledge

The Genesis narrative, therefore, and the conclusions of science as to the age and origin of the universe, of Earth, and of life, including human life, belong to two interactive but distinct aspects of human understanding. Genesis should be interpreted as saying very little, if anything, of relevance today about the age and mode of origin of Earth and living things. The story of creation is a prelude to the story of Adam and Eve's fall and the consequent human estrangement from God. As salvation history, its message is a religious one.

Those who misrepresent the Bible as a scientific presentation, rather than as a theological document, are destructive of sound religion. Religious people have no reason to fear the results of scientific research, because these results cannot contradict authentic religious experience. It is important for both religious people and scientists (by no means exclusive categories) to be clear about the differences between science and theology. Confusion on the part of creation science, of politicians, and of the general public bodes ill not only for the quality of science education but also for the good name of religion among thinking people.

Creation science at the local, regional, and state level has demonstrated that it is capable of, if not adept at, circumventing existing legislation. Laws alone are not enough to halt the restrictive measures that in practice limit the teaching of legitimate science and to exclude the teaching of pseudoscientific creation science *as science*. The problem is a cultural one with important educational implications.

Scientists cannot address this problem through science teaching alone. It seems to me that if creation science advocates and others who reject evolution, as well as an ancient age for Earth, are going to be reached at all, it will be by teachers who can address themselves to both kinds of knowledge, scientific and theological.[30]

The education of every science teacher who is likely to face the creation science mindset should include something about the premises and procedures of modern biblical scholarship and the distinct roles of scientific knowledge and religious faith. The Bible has a very special place in our culture, and even students from fundamentalist backgrounds are often pleasantly surprised and relieved to learn that there are sound methods of interpreting the Bible that in no way conflict with science.

A sound and critical analysis of Genesis makes it clear that the authors of that book had as their main objective to produce a history of Israel that provided a religious message and guidelines to an intimate relationship with the personal God who made a covenant with Israel. It is equally clear from other considerations that the role of science is to investigate the universe, including Earth, and to understand how it came to be as it is. Religious people who believe that God is the creator of the universe and the author of those laws by which it operates should find no conflict between science and religion.

Notes

1 National Academy of Sciences 1999.
2 National Academy of Sciences 1990.
3 van Beuren 1999.
4 Pennock 1999.
5 Gilkey 1985.
6 Ibid.
7 Stanley 1993.
8 Morris 1976.
9 Gilkey 1985.
10 Ibid.
11 Heidel 1951.
12 After Heidel 1951.
13 Maly 1968.
14 Vawter 1977.
15 Alter 1996.
16 Morris 1983.
17 Skehan 1986.
18 Gould 1977.
19 Brice 1982.
20 Lyell 1830.
21 Press and Siever 1993.
22 Ibid.
23 Ibid.
24 Ibid.
25 Bowring et al. 1993.
26 Stanley 1993.
27 Ibid.
28 Skehan 1986.
29 Stanley 1993.
30 Skehan 1983, Nelson this volume.

References

Alter, R. 1996. *Genesis*. New York: W.W. Norton & Company.

Bowring, S.A., J.P. Grotzinger, C.E. Isachsen, A.H. Knoll, C.M. Pelechaty, and P. Kolosov. 1993. Calibrating rates of early Cambrian evolution. *Science* 261: 1293–1298.

Brice, W.R. 1982. Bishop Ussher, John Lightfoot, and the age of creation. *Journal of Geological Education* 30: 18–24.

Darwin, C. 1859. *On the Origin of Species*. London: John Murray.

Gilkey, L. 1985. *Creationism on Trial: Evolution and God at Little Rock*. San Francisco: Harper and Row Publishers.

Gould, S J. 1977. *Ever Since Darwin: Reflections in Natural History*. New York: W.W. Norton.

Heidel, A. 1951. *The Babylonian Genesis*. Chicago: University of Chicago Press.

Lyell, C. 1830. *Principles of Geology*. Volume 1. New York: D. Appleton and Company.

Maly, E.H. 1968. Genesis, In *The Jerusalem Biblical Commentary*, edited by R.E. Brown, J.A. Fitzmyer S.J., R.E. Murphy O.Carm. New York: Prentice Hall, Inc.

Morris, H.M. 1976. *The Genesis Record: A Scientific and Devotional Commentary on the Book of Beginnings*. Grand Rapids, Michigan: Baker Book House.

————1983. Creationism, Evolutionism, and Liberal Theology—letter to the editor, *Journal of Geological Education*, 32: 143.

National Academy of Sciences. 1984. *Science and Creationism*. First edition. Washington, D.C., National Academy Press.

————1999. *Science and Creationism: A View from the National Academy of Sciences*. Second edition. Washington, D.C., National Academy Press.

Pennock, R.T. 1999. *Tower of Babel: The Evidence Against the New Creationism*. Cambridge, MA: M.I.T. Press.

Press, F., and R. Siever. 1993. *Earth*. New York: W.H. Freeman.

Skehan S.J., J.W. 1983. Theological basis for a Judeo-Christian position on creationism, *Journal of Geological Education* 31: 307–314.

Skehan S.J., J. W. 1986. The age of the Earth, of life, and of mankind: Geology and biblical theory versus creationism, In *Science and Creation*, edited by R.W. Hanson. New York: Macmillan.

Stanley, S.M. 1993. *Exploration of Earth and Life Through Time*. New York: W.H. Freeman and Company.

van Beuren, V.V. 1999. Kansas rejects evolution: A response from the Geoscience community, *Geotimes* 44(10): 18–22.

Vawter, B. 1977. *On Genesis: A New Reading*. New York: Doubleday.

Effective Strategies for Teaching Evolution and Other Controversial Topics

Craig E. Nelson

As scientists and science teachers, we find ourselves in a paradoxical situation. The economy—and with it most people's income directly or indirectly—increasingly depends on the products of science. At the same time, much of the public either rejects or does not understand the central theories of science. We find this especially puzzling for those ideas such as evolution, for which the scientific support is both quite strong and quite easily understood.

A fundamental question for science education in the United States today is: How can we produce a scientifically literate society, especially in areas that are publicly controversial? I will discuss four groups of issues and problems that are central to our efforts to produce a scientifically literate society. I will also suggest some strategies that are important for addressing each of the issues and problems. My examination here of this question arrives at six central conclusions.

1. Active learning is even more important for controversial topics than for the rest of science.

2. One major source of our problems, and not just for publicly controversial issues, is that we too often teach science as a set of conclusions. We should instead teach science as a set of processes for thinking critically about alternatives.

3. We have good ways to judge the levels of strength of support for scientific theories and other criteria for comparing them. Helping students understand these ways of judging is integral to teaching science as critical thinking. It also allows us to show that a publicly controversial theory is not necessarily a scientifically weak or scientifically controversial theory.

4. Although evolution often is seen as problematical, it is scientifically as strong or stronger than any other major scientific theory. Interestingly, most other major

scientific theories probably are even less well understood by the public. They would be less well accepted than evolution if they were understood.

5. Public controversies usually rest on disagreements about consequences. Hence, the parties can rationally disagree on how strong the evidence must be to justify a particular decision. If students are to understand why topics such as evolution are controversial, we must help them understand the different views of consequences. Only then can they really make an intelligent decision among the options.

6. Students have strong expectations of what should happen in science classes. These expectations flow in part from their levels of intellectual development. Both the expectations and the levels must be taken into account in the ways we structure our approaches, especially for controversial issues.

Although evolution is my central example, several of the problems and strategies discussed here apply to many other controversial issues. I hope the juxtaposition of issues with strategies will help you consider additional applications and devise further teaching strategies. Table 1 lists the issues and problems, together with the strategies and key metaphors. Table 2 emphasizes the heterogeneity of religious views that underlie the origins controversy. Table 3 explores the interplay of uncertainty, scientific knowledge, and religious views, thus providing a map of many of the most important features of the origins controversy.

Problems That Arise from Traditional Pedagogy in Science

Studies of science education, and of teaching generally, repeatedly conclude that major changes are needed at all educational levels. Several recent reviews show us how teaching can be made much more effective, both in science and generally.[1]

A key finding is that didactic pedagogy and passive learning lead to much more limited and temporary understandings of science than can be produced with alternative, more active pedagogies. Because of the way college science is traditionally taught, it sometimes seems that active learning is less important in more advanced classes, even in secondary school. However, much of the most stunning recent evidence for the superiority of active learning has emerged at the college level.

Let me quite briefly summarize four key examples.

1. Hake's review[2] found that structured, student–student interaction approximately doubled the amount of Newtonian physics mastered in introductory physics courses—a conclusion that held across a wide array of institutions from high schools to Harvard. Most impressively, no lecturer matched the average gain achieved by courses that included interaction.

Table 1. Controversial Issues: Key Pedagogical Problems and Strategies

PROBLEMS THAT ARISE FROM TRADITIONAL PEDAGOGY IN SCIENCE	
Problem: Didactic pedagogy and passive learning lead to limited and temporary understanding of science.	**Strategy:** Emphasize active learning.

PROBLEMS THAT ARISE FROM TRADITIONAL CONTENT AND CURRICULA IN SCIENCE	
Problem: We often appear to present all topics in science as equally well supported, as "truth."	**Strategy:** Emphasize the wide variation in strength of support among different scientific ideas. See also next strategy. *Key Metaphor:* "Big-Burger".
Problem: In a rush to "cover the material," we often just present the conclusions, leaving out the underlying critical thinking.	**Strategy:** Emphasize science as a process of critical thinking. *Key Tool:* "Fair tests" of alternatives.
Problem: Often, we do not help students learn to compare the strengths of disparate scientific ideas. *Key Consequent Misconception:* Evolution is scientifically weak.	**Strategy:** Emphasize the distinction between fundamental empirical patterns and the causes that account for them. **Strategy:** Use history to compare disparate scientific accomplishments. *Key Comparison:* Darwin as the Newton of Biology. **Strategy:** Use criteria to compare great scientific ideas. *Key Comparison 1:* Einstein as the Darwin of Physics. *Key Comparison 2:* Evolution is as good as science gets!
Problem: We often use words in ways that are directly contradictory to common usage and, even, in ways that are inconsistent among various sciences. *Key Consequent Misconception:* Evolution is "just a theory."	**Strategy:** Use students' language to bypass the theory versus fact and other similar confusions. *Key Example:* If it is a fact that the planets orbit the Sun, then evolution is a stronger fact.

PROBLEMS THAT ARISE OUTSIDE TRADITIONAL PEDAGOGY AND CONTENT	
Problem: Public controversies usually rest on disagreements about consequences. Hence, the parties can rationally disagree on how strong the evidence must be to justify a particular decision.	**Strategy:** Explicitly examine the alternative views of consequences and tradeoffs as seen by the various parties. *Key Metaphor:* Rusty hand-grenade. **Strategy:** Bridge false dichotomies.
Problem: Students often want us to just tell them what to memorize.	**Strategy:** Teach the "game" of science. **Strategy:** Draw a clear distinction between what science does and what religion does. **Strategy:** Focus on humans.

2. Springer, et al[3] recently reviewed "the effects of small group learning on undergraduates in science, mathematics, engineering, and technology." The average effect on achievement "would move a student from the 50th percentile to the 70th percentile on a standardized test." They also found strong effects on persistence and on students' attitudes toward science.

3. Angelo and Cross[4] report a calculus course in which writing and structured discussion were able to eliminate the grade of F completely, with no reduction in standards. An economist reported similar results to me—no F's in three years—with the students assessed against nine other sections using common mid-term and final exams.

4. Treisman found that he could reduce the D and F rate for African-Americans in calculus from about 60 percent to about 4 percent with structured active learning. Again, this gain was achieved with no reduction in standards.[5]

Like these examples, the literature on the effects of structured student–student interaction and other forms of active learning usually shows large, positive effects on student learning, especially in science and math courses. These effects are so strong that to teach without using at least an admixture of active approaches is to knowingly sacrifice learning. The first problem and strategy follow from this.

Problem: Didactic pedagogy and passive learning lead to limited and temporary understanding of science.

Active learning is especially important for issues that the students see as controversial. There are at least two fundamental reasons.

First, these issues often involve a series of alternative conceptions or nonscientific misconceptions. The use of active learning is especially important when such conceptions are already in place.

Second, dealing with controversies effectively requires that students learn to think in more complex ways.[6] Active learning is a key tool here, too. This leads to the first global strategy for improving the effectiveness of science education, especially for controversial issues.

Strategy: Emphasize active learning.

I have placed this strategy first to emphasize its fundamental role. Each of the other strategies will be more effective when implemented using active learning.

However, a key issue in using active learning is deciding what goals we are seeking to achieve. The rest of this article is designed to help teachers define these goals and to help them understand the intellectual steps that students must attain to move toward the selected goals. Within this area, I suggest just a few of the many key ways to apply active learning.

For both evolution and the nature of science, my colleagues and I work extensively with high school teachers to develop active learning lessons. We have made many of these available on the Internet, together with links to other sites containing similar lessons.[7] Further explorations of the ties I see between the use of active learning strategies, especially collaborative learning, and fostering critical thinking are available elsewhere.[8]

Problems That Arise from Traditional Content and Curricula in Science

A second thrust in the literature on improving learning in science courses compliments the earlier focus on active learning. This second thrust emphasizes that traditional curricular and content also need to be reconsidered. The four problems in this group are self-inflicted. That is, they are the predictable results of the traditional ways of addressing the content of science and of organizing curricula.

This is encouraging. Just as we as teachers have the power to alter our pedagogy to make learning more active, so we have the power to alter the content of our courses. We can increase the extent to which we focus on the underlying processes of reasoning and comparison. This will make understanding the nature of science the route to a deeper and more genuine understanding of science itself.

Problem: We often appear to present all topics in science as equally well supported.

As scientists and science teachers, we are charmed by the patterns of nature and their explanations, and we want to share as many of these as possible with our students. In the process, we often present them as simply factual and don't take time to help our students understand the radically different degrees of evidence and other support for different scientific ideas. This problem is amplified both by cultural images of scientific knowledge as absolute and by students' limited sophistication.

Strategy: Emphasize the wide variation in strength of support among different scientific ideas.

Key Metaphor: "Big-Burger"

The first solution is to help students identify and understand the wide variation in the strengths of support for different scientific ideas. This is especially easy for questions of origins (of the universe, of life, of consciousness), as the strength of support is so radically different from that for normal science. These differences are summarized by a double-decker hamburger metaphor for the history of the natural world (illustration p. 24 and Table 3 p. 38).

In a "Big-Burger" sandwich, the three layers of bun, like much American white bread, are airy and very soft and compressible. These three layers can be matched with the three origins questions, on which there currently are no solid scientific answers, only somewhat-informed, somewhat-airy speculation.

1. Let the bottom layer of bun correspond with our somewhat airy answers to the question of how the universe got started (see illustration below).

2. The middle layer of bun then corresponds with our answers to the question of how a genetic system evolved (with tRNA in the middle of a largely arbitrary translation system being a special difficulty).

3. The top layer of bun, in turn, represents the answers, airy once again, to the question of how consciousness arises out of molecular reactions.

Between these three layers of metaphorical bun, there are two big layers of meaty science (illustration below and Table 3 p. 38). Specifically, we have comparatively solid answers for how and often why the physical universe changed from when big bang was well underway on through the formation of elements, organic molecules, solar systems, and planets. Similarly, once a functioning genetic system is in place, we have strong answers for how and often why organisms changed.

Emphasizing these differences in strength of support between airy and meaty realms in science leads naturally to the next question. How do scientists distinguish speculation from solid knowledge?

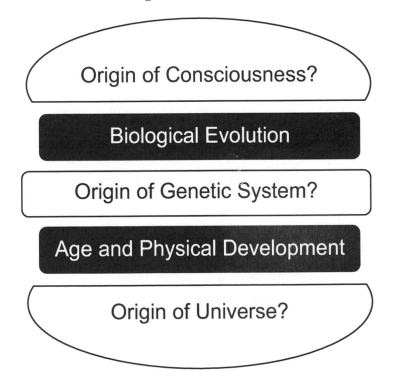

An expanded version of each of these layers is provided in Table 3.

Problem: In "covering the material," we often present just the conclusions, leaving out the underlying critical thinking.

Several major studies have emphasized that science teachers at all levels overemphasize content and pay too little attention to helping students understand the processes of scientific critical thinking.[9] Although the essence of science is evidence-based critical thinking, in a rush to "cover the material" we often present just the conclusions. This reduces science to memorization and hides the underlying analytical processes.

Strategy: Emphasize science as a process of critical thinking.

What is critical thinking in science? Let's start with a basic model. Scientists first develop alternative patterns or explanations. They then use evidence and other appropriate criteria to distinguish the better from the weaker. For example, in the 1880s three hypotheses on Earth's age were popular:

1. A few thousand years old (from biblical genealogies)

2. A maximum of 20–100 million years old (Lord Kelvin, from cooling rates)

3. Several hundreds of millions of years old (geologists, from rates of erosion, etc.).

Fair tests of these three alternatives were needed.

Fair tests of alternatives. A fair test is based on a line of evidence different from those on which the alternatives were proposed. Ideally, this new line of evidence could turn out to have supported any of these alternatives. Radioactive dating provided just such a test for the age of the Earth. None of the alternatives had used it as a foundation, and, it could have shown that Earth's rocks were all less than 20,000 years old or less than 100 million years old. Instead, it showed the oldest are four billion years old. Many other lines of physical evidence provide similar fair tests, and their results uniformly support an age for Earth of billions of years.[10] This, therefore, is a very strong conclusion.

As a second example, suppose you were living in the 1840s in Great Britain when the geological column was first put in order. What changes, if any, should we have expected in fossils from the oldest to the youngest? Alternative hypotheses supported by ideas other than evolution included all kinds of organisms in the oldest rocks (with or without subsequent extinction); cycles among dominant groups; and successive independent elaborations and extinctions. Thus, Darwin proposed evolution despite, not because of, the fossil record. In *On the Origin of Species*[11] he had to treat the fossil record as a major problem. The oldest marine fossil beds then known contained most of the modern marine phyla. Darwin predicted that, if his theory were true, life had to have begun with a few very simple forms. The record itself provided a fair test of this and the alternative hypotheses. Our discoveries of much older fossils confirmed Darwin's prediction and showed that the alternatives were largely wrong.

Most science should be taught in this way. We should start first by helping the students explore alternative patterns or processes, and only later help them examine the evidence and other criteria that allow a choice among the alternatives. The ideal settings for the development of such understanding are authentic laboratory or field problems where students develop hypotheses, design experimental treatments and controls, gather and analyze the data, and defend their conclusions.

This comparative approach emphatically does not mean that all of the ideas should be treated as equivalent in quality. On the contrary, learning should be structured so that students deeply understand the processes of science. Then, their mastery of fair tests and other evidence and criteria will allow them to understand which ideas are strong, which are suggestive, and which are not defensible. The strongest ideas in science are those, like an old Earth and evolution, that repeatedly emerge as better when challenged with multiple empirical questions as fair tests.

Problem: Often, we do not help students learn to compare the strengths of disparate scientific ideas. This leaves them free to think that publicly controversial ideas are somehow weaker than "good" science.

Typically we do not help students understand how scientists decide which accomplishments are great science and which are routine. We usually offer the major sciences in separate courses. Even when we integrate them, we frequently ask the students to make few, if any, comparisons among them. This leaves students free to think that publicly controversial ideas such as evolution are somehow weaker than scientific ideas that are not as controversial (e.g., gravitational theory).

How can we compare the ideas of, say, Newton and Darwin? History can be of considerable help, especially when coupled with a distinction between patterns and processes.

Two strategies: Emphasize the distinction between fundamental empirical patterns and the causes that account for them, and use history to compare disparate scientific accomplishments.

The distinction between major empirical patterns (e.g., planetary orbits) and the causes (e.g., inertia and gravity, warped space) that account for them is crucial in understanding science. But we often fail to keep this distinction clear. For example, we use the term "evolution" to mean the empirical patterns that show how we and other eukaryotes evolved from simpler forms. We also use it to mean the processes that explain those patterns, especially heredity and selection. Let's examine the distinction between patterns and processes a bit further.

Patterns. Scientists ask what inferred patterns the data support. For example, the planets orbit the Sun in irregular ellipses. This pattern had to be inferred: No one ever saw a planet (except, arguably, Mercury) orbit the Sun, and the outer planets move so slowly that some have not orbited the Sun even once since they were discovered. We had to infer the patterns from the regularities in the data. This was, in part, Copernicus' contribution.

Processes. Science seeks a set of empirically validated processes that explain why particular patterns occur and, consequently, why other patterns do not. The distinction between patterns and processes allows us to draw important historical parallels between the development of our explanations for the motion of the planets around the Sun and the development of our explanations for the evolution of life on Earth.

Newton's key contribution was to show that the planets orbit the Sun in irregular ellipses due to the interactions of inertia and gravitation. Newton thus explained Copernicus' planetary patterns. Similarly, Darwin explained patterns summarized earlier by Linneaus and Paley (Table 3).

Further, Newton showed the ellipses have to be imperfect (distorted) where the planets affect each other's orbits. He thus explained both the ellipses and the deviations from perfectly elliptical. Similarly, Darwin showed both that natural selection could explain the ways in which organisms have adapted (Paley's emphasis) and that inheritance for common ancestors could explain vestigial organs and other "whole great classes" of ways in which organisms were not perfectly adapted.

In these fundamental and very important ways, Darwin was the Newton of biology. He used inheritance and natural selection to explain patterns discovered earlier. Such comparisons help students (and us) understand why only some very strongly supported ideas are truly great.

Again, active pedagogy matters. These ideas will more powerfully shape students' scientific world-views when they "discover" them, wrestle with them in a collaborative setting, and consolidate the meaning through the facilitated development of a group consensus.

Strategy: Use criteria to compare great scientific ideas.

The previous strategies allow us to use historical perspectives to compare, for example, Darwin's accomplishments with those of Newton. A complimentary strategy is to ask how we determine the comparative strength of major contemporary scientific theories.

Is evolutionary theory currently much weaker than, about as strong as, or much stronger than other major scientific theories such as relativity? Because major theories address quite different things, data and fair tests do not allow a direct comparison. We need a different set of criteria. Here are eight criteria for comparing major scientific theories.

1. How many lines of independent evidence support the theory?
Relativity, for example, is supported by only a few lines of independent evidence. Several more lines support both evolution (Table 3) and plate tectonics (earthquake distributions, sea-floor spreading, ages of oceanic islands, etc.).[12] Because each of

these theories has very strong empirical support, we would need an alternative theory with approximately equal empirical support before we would consider rejecting it.

2. How many previously unconnected areas of knowledge did a theory tie together? Bronowski[13] provides another criterion for comparing scientific accomplishments. He suggests we examine the historical significance of the multiple lines of evidence. Newton's accomplishment, he explains, lay in connecting two things that everyone knew to be different: the motions of celestial bodies (moons) and those of terrestrial objects (cannonballs and apples). Einstein, of course, made even more connections, linking together space, time, matter, and energy. However, his synthesis followed Darwin's equally spectacular connection of evolutionary history with the Linnaean hierarchy, with differences in the distribution of organisms, the patterns of compromises in adaptation, and many more facets of biology (Table 3). In this sense, connecting several fundamentally different groups of natural phenomena, Einstein was the Darwin of physics.

3. Does the theory make precise predictions? Major scientific theories make many predictions, both basic and applied. For evolution, my favorite predictions include two from Darwin: that life had to have begun with a few quite simple forms and that fossils connecting humans to chimpanzees and gorillas would be found in Africa. Predicting the development of resistance to pesticides and antibiotics is also straightforward given basic evolutionary theory.

One of the most important kinds of predictions in science is the prediction of what we will not find (i.e., of what is not possible). Triangular planetary orbits are an example of a phenomenon that is impossible under our physical theories. Darwin's explanation of classification lets us make similarly strong predictions. For example, because mammals and birds originated from very separate and disparate taxa of reptiles, we can predict that no intermediates between bats (or other mammals) and birds will ever be found in the fossil record. Similarly, most of the organisms you might imagine by combining traits (snakes with feathered wings, for example) cannot have existed, as they combine traits from separate evolutionary lineages. Thus, they will never be found either in the jungle or in the fossil record.

4. How clear are the causal mechanisms? Newton renamed "falling tendency" as "gravity" without explaining how it acts causally. This is still unexplained, leading to current searches for gravity waves. Besides natural selection, the major causal agent in Darwin's theory was the tendency of organisms to resemble their parents and more remote ancestors. As with falling tendency, the causal basis of this resembling tendency was then unknown.

Now, however, resemblance to ancestors is clearly a physical necessity. Each organism's DNA is a copy of that of its parents and, in turn, of more remote ancestors. The causal basis of evolution is more deeply understood than is the causal basis of relativity (and than that of plate tectonics).[14] Thus, on this criterion evolution is the stronger theory.

5. Does the theory adequately explain the ultimate origin of the sys-

tems it describes and explains? Workers with all theories sometimes attempt to examine the origins of the systems they study. Neither relativity nor quantum mechanics adequately explains the ultimate origin of the physical universe. Plate tectonics does not explain the origin of Earth. Thus, the fact that evolution does not adequately explain the origin of life does not make it any weaker than other major scientific theories.

6. Is the theory scientifically controversial, or only publicly or politically controversial? Each major theory discussed has essentially universal scientific acceptance. Most surprising was the rapid acceptance of plate tectonics in the late 1960s, once sea-floor spreading was verified.[15]

Controversies within science that address major, well-supported theories usually address what the public would see as quite minor points. For example, there have been heated debates in biology in the last couple of decades over classification. Thus: Should we maintain reptiles as a separate, intact group now that it is clear that some reptiles (crocodiles and dinosaurs) are more closely related to birds than they are to other reptiles (turtles)? These current controversies within evolution address the details of evolutionary history and the details of causal mechanisms. None of them question the occurrence or extent of evolution itself.

7. Is the theory fundamental to many practical benefits embraced by our economic system? Each major theory has important economic benefits. Evolution is of growing importance in the development of medical treatments. Examples include the identification of the sources of particular HIV strains and even individual infections (thus facilitating control)[16]; the use of geographic and taxonomic regularities in the search for natural compounds that yield new medicines; and the recent emergence of "Darwinian medicine."[17]

8. Is the theory widely understood and accepted by the general public? It appears that no major theory is widely understood and accepted by the general public. Plate tectonics requires an acceptance of an old Earth. Yet, polls repeatedly show that a plurality of American adults believes in a young Earth. Relativity requires that we understand, among other things, that the faster we move the slower time actually runs. This effect is large enough to affect our ability to control artificial satellites.[18] Quantum mechanics is even weirder. Does the general public understand and accept that when you smash your finger between a nail and a hammer, all three "objects" are almost pure space? Or that Earth itself is almost empty space. The entire Earth, if placed in the gravitational field at the surface of a neutron star, would fit inside a large stadium!

In summary, according to each of these eight criteria, evolution is as good as or better than the other major scientific theories. Evolution is as good as great science gets! Because evolution is sometimes portrayed as scientifically marginal, some may be surprised (as I initially was) by my conclusion that evolution is as strong as any other major scientific idea. Committees formed by the National Academy of Science have twice addressed this issue and have reached similar conclusions.[19] My conclusion that none of the major theories of science are understood and accepted by the general public underlies my urging that all of science, not just the controversial parts, should be taught in ways like those illustrated here for evolution.

Problem: We often use words in ways that are contradictory to common usage and even in ways that are inconsistent among various sciences.

Again, the problem here is of our own making. In science, we often use words in ways that are directly contradictory to common usage and even in ways that are inconsistent among various sciences. Theory and fact provide an important example.

In general conversation, "theory" often is used to mean "unsupported speculations." But in science, "theory" is used only for ideas that have exceptionally strong support. Similarly, in general conversation, "fact" typically means a direct observation, one that is absolutely beyond doubt. For example: You are reading this sentence right now. "Fact" in science typically refers to a very strongly supported conclusion derived from a group of observations. Typically, such conclusions are not absolutely beyond doubt and, occasionally, scientific facts have turned out to be wrong. Birds and dinosaurs were placed in quite different groups. This "fact" has had to be revised as it became apparent that birds are the direct descendants either of dinosaurs or of their close allies.

These inconsistencies in the way we use words become especially problematical for issues that the public regards as controversial. For these, they allow anyone who dislikes a scientific idea to refer to it as "just a theory."

Strategy: Use students' language to bypass the theory versus fact confusion.

The fact versus theory confusion becomes manageable once we have made a clear distinction between patterns and processes and know how to compare the strength of ideas about disparate areas of science. More numerous, strong, distinct lines of evidence show that large scale evolution has occurred (Table 3) than show that the planets orbit the Sun. Therefore, if it is a "fact" that the planets go around the Sun, then evolution is a stronger fact. Alternatively, if evolution is a "theory," then the idea that the planets go around the Sun is a theory also, but a weaker one. Best, both can be considered (like the rest of the core of science) as very strongly supported, inferred facts.

Two Problems That Arise from Outside Traditional Pedagogy and Content

We have thus far considered a set of problems that exists in science education related to how we traditionally teach science and its content, and how we organize science curricula. In addition, we have considered a number of strategies that can allow us to appreciably increase students' understanding of the various sciences and their comparative strengths, as well as the nature and power of science.

We are now ready to look at two additional dimensions of public controversies involving science and strategies for addressing these. The first problem follows from the contrast between the consequences emphasized in basic science and those that must be considered for real-world decisions. It is thus a result of how we usually think about science rather than of conscious pedagogical choices. The second problem reflects the need for further intellectual growth by our students.

These two problems make it necessary to design additional strategies to teach publicly controversial issues more effectively. They may even broaden our view of the kinds of material that are legitimately included in science courses. On the other hand, without such strategies, we may omit or underemphasize the pertinent science.

Problem: Public controversies usually rest on disagreements about consequences. Hence, the parties can rationally disagree on how strong the evidence must be to justify a particular decision.

If a theory is strong scientifically, does that mean one rationally must—or even should—accept it? The controversies surrounding the teaching of evolution can help us understand additional reasons why much of the public is skeptical of science and, specifically, of evolution. The core of the problem here is that real-world decisions involve consequences and values, and different groups will see different sets of consequences as fundamentally important.

Within basic science, the acceptance of a new hypothesis is based largely on the strength with which the supporting data allow a rejection of the null hypothesis. The null hypothesis is, roughly, the best alternative to the hypothesis being examined. Conventionally, acceptance of a new hypothesis follows whenever the chance that the null hypothesis can account for the differences between two sets of data drops below 5 percent (less than 1 chance in 20).

Again, within basic science, we seldom need to remember the underlying tradeoffs, but they are still there. For example, if we used 10 percent instead of 5 percent as our standard for rejecting the null, two consequences would follow. Research would be cheaper and quicker, as smaller sample sizes would suffice. The tradeoff would be an increase in the proportion of published studies that were based on spurious results. With 1 percent, alternatively, the proportion of spurious published studies would decrease, but then research would be more expensive and take longer, as greater replication would be needed.

Five percent is a somewhat arbitrary compromise among these tradeoffs. If, however, real-world consequences are important, an arbitrary acceptance of 5 percent will almost never be appropriate. The level of support—strength of data—that is adequate for one to reasonably accept an idea depends on tradeoffs. Specifically it depends on tradeoffs between the benefits that follow if the hypothesis turns out to be correct versus the consequences that follow if we accept the hypothesis and it turns out to be wrong. The difference between basic and applied science is that real-world consequences are conventionally ignored in basic science but often not ignored in applied science. Further, public controversies involving scientific issues almost always involve conflicting perceptions of consequences and their value. For any publicly controversial area of science, a key strategy is to help students understand and discuss these differences in perceived consequences.

Strategy: Explicitly examine the alternative views of consequences and tradeoffs as seen by the various parties.

 The various parties in public controversies involving scientific issues often disagree about the consequences and their relative importance, as in the controversies over evolution. They then may rationally disagree on how strong the evidence must be to justify a particular decision. A discussion focused simply on the strength of data and other scientific support can be largely irrelevant. Put bluntly, the data aren't the only thing that should determine what ideas we accept. This is so contrary to the usual mind-set in science that we must start with a concrete metaphor.

Key Metaphor: Rusty Hand-Grenade.

Consider, for example, an intact but quite rusty hand-grenade one finds from an old military storehouse. With it on the table between us, we agree that it is so rusty that the chances of it exploding if we pull the pin are slim—decidedly less than one in 10 thousand. Let us further say that one of us has sufficient munitions expertise that the one in 10 thousand is an informed judgment, not just a wild guess. Shall we pull the pin?

The most probable hypothesis, by far, is that the grenade will not explode. When presented with this thought experiment, however, most people conclude that we should not pull the pin. Why not? Because, if the most probable hypothesis is wrong and the grenade does go off, the results are likely to be "inconvenient," especially for those testing the hypothesis. It is important, too, that a demonstration that the grenade is too rusty to explode has negligible benefits. Thus, it is totally rational to reject even a very probable hypothesis when the benefits of acceptance, were it true, are small, and the consequences of being wrong are large.

Differing Views of Consequence. Scientists and science teachers typically understand that the evidence supporting evolution is exceedingly strong (Table 3), so that it is very probably correct in its broad conclusions. Within the set of consequences usually considered by basic science, any rejection seems quite irrational.

Many fundamentalist Christians, Jews, and Muslims bring a quite different framework to bear. A central difference is in the answer to the question: What are the consequences of accepting evolution, should it ultimately be false? Evolution by far is currently the best-supported scientific hypothesis. Hence, the answer, within the framework of science, is that the consequences are negligible—we know that ideas in science have to be modified through time, sometimes radically.

However, within the framework used by many religious fundamentalists, premature acceptance of evolution, should it be false, is a serious mistake. Through its perceived conflict with Genesis, it increases the risk of rejecting the truth of scripture and, thus, the chance of eternal damnation. Given the fundamentalists' assumptions, the rejection of evolution, despite otherwise overwhelming evidence is as rational as our refusal to pull the pin on a rusty grenade.

This perspective first became clear to me as I sought to understand the controversies surrounding nuclear power.[19] Most public controversies, including those in which scientific issues play a role, have contrasting views of consequences at their core.

More on Consequences? Getting students in a science class to consider consequence is a major advance. It makes clear that the core issues are not scientific but center on consequences and how we value them. Some would say that we should leave further analysis to social science or even religious studies classes. Science teachers who are uncomfortable with some of the following (or preceding) approaches certainly should not use them.

However, if a teacher is comfortable exploring contrasts in consequences just a bit deeper, three major advantages can accrue. The rusty hand-grenade analogy leaves science contrasted with religion. This apparent contrast misrepresents most religious thinking in the United States. Further, such a dichotomous choice leaves students with little room to develop, and may cause them to reject science altogether. Rejection of science is clearly not the best outcome if we want to increase public understanding of science. Finally, to leave the students with a choice between science or religion is to abandon the task of teaching critical thinking at exactly the point where real progress is possible. This is especially unfortunate as evolution provides a topic where student interest will often sustain the hard work necessary for intellectual development.

The following approaches help us achieve these deeper goals. They focus on ways to help students attain a richer understanding of the alternatives, and of the benefits and consequences of accepting and rejecting them. Such an understanding of intermediate positions typically requires looking further at differing opinions about the consequences outside of science. I carefully emphasize, both here and with my students, that what I am doing is sociological description. I also carefully avoid arguing for any particular set of such consequences, or for any particular underlying set of religious beliefs. Analogues to this set of approaches can also be applied widely to understanding—and teaching about—other publicly controversial aspects of science.

Strategy: Bridge false dichotomies.

Most public controversies rapidly become inappropriately polarized. Casting the issue as religious creationism versus atheistic science is a common example. Since this false distinction serves the political interests of young-Earth creationists, it has received much public press. Consequently, even many college students think that most U.S. churches oppose evolution and are quite surprised to learn otherwise. Thus, one effective response to false dichotomies is to help students understand that intermediate positions are held by many respectable people. This approach is greatly facilitated when we provide opportunities for safe, reasoned, discussions.

I will briefly list four tools for bridging dichotomies in the case of creation and evolution. Each can be used as a focus for such discussions.

1. The article by Skehan in this volume is an excellent tool for helping us under-

Table 2. Evolution and Creation: From a Dichotomy to a Gradient

NON-THEISTIC EVOLUTION [THE BASIC STANCE OF SCIENCE]
Accepts: Old Earth, normal geology and evolution.   • Scientific questions should be decided independently of religious assumptions: Religion has been of no help in deciding either patterns (e.g., shape of orbits) or their causes. Similarly, arguments either for or against God that use natural patterns or processes as evidence are also logically flawed.
GRADUAL CREATION (THEISTIC EVOLUTION)
Accepts: Old Earth, normal geology and evolution.   • Evolution is God's way of making diverse organisms (just as gravitation is God's way of controlling planetary motion).   • Creation is the ultimate origin of the universe and continues at each moment in its maintenance.   • Some versions emphasize the independent creation of life or of souls. Others also suggest that evidence of intelligent design can be seen in particular features of life or of the universe.
PROGRESSIVE CREATION
Accepts: Old earth and normal geology but only limited evolution.   • Like gradual creation, except that it accepts only evolution within groups.   • New groups (especially humans) were newly created at approximately the time when they first appear in fossil record. The diversity and complexity of new forms when created increases progressively through time.
QUICK CREATION
• The Earth is only a few thousand years old. The geological record was largely formed in a year-long global flood. Some adaptive variation has occurred, but only within "kind."   • This position rejects or misinterprets much of the physical and biological sciences.   • Quick creation is often mislabeled as creationism or scientific creationism. Gradual and progressive creation are both decidedly more scientific *and* are equally dependent on a Creator.

stand the legitimacy and importance of intermediate positions. Anyone who feels that science and religion cannot be reconciled should give his article a very careful read. I also recommend it as a tool for talking with troubled students.

2. A powerful tool for moderating the students' tendency to think that the only options are the polarized ones is to give students a list of positions in the controversy or, better but more time consuming, to ask students to develop such a list. For options surrounding evolution, listing several creationist positions (Table 2) allows small group discussion focused on "if you are a creationist, what type of creationist are you and why?"

3. To briefly emphasize the legitimacy of such intermediate positions, teachers might find it fruitful to ask students to familiarize themselves with the list of plaintiffs who opposed an Arkansas law that "public schools within this state shall give balanced treatment to creation-science and to evolution-science." Judge Overton's decision[21] declared the law unconstitutional and listed the plaintiffs:

The individual plaintiffs [who ask that the law be overturned] include the resident Arkansas Bishops of the United Methodist, Episcopal, Roman Catholic and African Methodist Episcopal Churches, the principal official of the Presbyterian Churches in Arkansas, other United Methodist, Southern Baptist, and Presbyterian clergy . . .

I use this case after I share the parallel between rusty grenades and the position of many fundamentalists on evolution. This example makes it easy to ask why so many churches would oppose the Arkansas law.

4. What opposing tradeoff might balance the risk to salvation that the fundamentalists emphasize? Full statements of various American Churches in support of evolution have been compiled and are readily accessible either for class use or as a resource for troubled students.[22] These are a good complement to Skehan's article.

My favorite statement, and one of the most succinct and ancient, is from Saint Augustine's *On the Literal Meaning of Genesis*:

Usually, even a non-Christian knows something about the Earth, the heavens, and the other elements of this world... Now, it is a disgraceful and dangerous thing for an infidel to hear a Christian, presumably giving the meaning of Holy Scripture, talking nonsense on these topics; and we should take all means to prevent such an embarrassing situation... The shame is... that people outside the household of faith think our sacred writers held such opinions... If they find a Christian mistaken in a field which they themselves know well and hear him maintaining his foolish opinions about our books, how are they going to believe those books in matters concerning the resurrection of the dead, the hope of eternal life, and the kingdom of heaven...?

It was evident at least as early as 400 A.D. that there is a risk to faith from denying strongly supported ideas about the natural world. And Augustine emphasizes that this risk can partially or wholly counterbalance any risk from questioning particular interpretations of Genesis. This counterbalancing risk adds a strong religious justification to the already strong scientific justification for rejecting the young-Earth and flood geology interpretations.

Problem: Students often want us to just tell them what to memorize.

As emphasized earlier, a central goal in teaching science should be to help students understand how scientists decide which ideas are better and which are weaker. A contrasting preference for dichotomies reflects many students' (and adults') level of cognitive development.[23] Students' prior school experience often has conditioned them to prefer dichotomies and "truth." They ache for us to just tell them what to memorize. Often, they are impatient with our attempts to focus on the underlying reasoning. Further, they are likely to think that if no perfect truth is available, then all answers are really just equivalent opinions. This problem is compounded when students consider nonscientific consequences important. One strategy addresses both aspects.

Strategy: Teach the "game" of science.

Ask students to understand and explain which scientists accept and on the basis of what criteria—whether or not that is what the students themselves think. For example, ask them to investigate and explain why evolution is good science. The key addition to the previous strategies is to say explicitly that the task is not to believe or accept the science, but rather to understand the "game" of science. This only seems fair. Students should understand clearly why scientists accept an idea before deciding whether to accept it themselves.

The students often feel that if one has to compare ideas, then all alternatives must be equally valid. Asking them to understand the "game" of science challenges this stance but seems not to be so threatening. Asking them to understand alternative views of consequences promotes the development of further sophistication. Doing so also helps them acquire sympathetic insight into others' perspectives. Such insight is key to the kinds of intellectual development that should happen in learning science, but typically do not.[24] The sympathetic insight also fosters a more civilized class by helping students who accept one point of view (such as evolution or quick creation) be more understanding of others' views.

Here again, pedagogy matters. A modeling of patient listening and reasoned response by the teacher, rather than outright dismissal, is vital.

Strategy: Draw a clear distinction between what science does and what religion does.

A second strategy also helps make the game of science clear. Emphasize what science does not do, as well as what it does. Continuing with an example developed earlier: Many people would like to say that God makes the planets orbit the Sun in irregular ellipses due to the interaction of inertia and gravitation.

Science is of no help in deciding whether one should append "God makes" to the explanation. This is one of the roles of religion. Similarly, religion has been of no help for the core tasks of science. Religion does not help us determine the patterns (irregular ellipses or circles or squares), nor does it help us decide among the causal factors. Put differently, "God made it so" does not provide an explanation in the scientific sense; this reasoning is compatible, for example, with orbits of any shape (triangles or perfect circles, etc.). Newton's laws in contrast can explain only certain patterns (i.e., rough ellipses). They are not compatible with others, thus excluding perfect ellipses, circles, etc.

Strategy: Focus on humans.

For evolution, the evidence that Darwin compiled in support of a common ancestry of humans and apes was already quite strong. In recent decades the molecular, paleontological, and behavioral evidence[25] also has become very strong. If the acceptance of scientific ideas was simply a function of the strength of scientific evidence, human evolution would be widely embraced. On the contrary, for many students human evolution is one of the most troublesome aspects of evolution, leading some to accept the evolution of all forms except humans. But virtually all students are quite interested in the details of evidence for human evolution. Nickels[26] develops well the advantages of focusing on human evolution and describes several approaches for doing so.

Throughout science, a similar focus on the applications of science to human biology and on important applied problems usually increases student interest radically. Again in a rush for coverage, we often allocate little time for this focus. But these are typically the consequences that students regard as most important. By emphasizing them, we increase students' motivation to do the mental work necessary for questioning old positions and for cognitive growth.

Summary

Much of the public either doesn't understand or rejects many central theories of modern science. Some of the underlying problems are predictable results of traditional ways of teaching science. Others involve diverse views of the consequences of particular publicly controversial ideas. In both cases, powerful pedagogical strategies are available for our use. Although evolution has been my central example, most of the strategies apply to many publicly controversial issues and, indeed, to teaching most of science.

Areas of science that traditionally have not seen much challenge are now also becoming publicly controversial. The challenges by antievolutionists range well outside biology to encompass much of the core of physics and geology. The recent flourishing of "intelligent design" arguments, summarized and critiqued well by Pennock,[27] make the challenges to the naturalistic base of all science much more explicit. Strahler[28] provides a superlative summary of many Creationist arguments and of their scientific limitations. His book is the most important source for teachers where evolution is challenged by fundamentalist groups. The National Center for Science Education is also a major source of support in such cases.

The strategies I have presented here focus largely on modifying the content we present. Changes in the way we teach, especially the increased use of active and hands-on learning and abundant opportunities for dialogue, even in lecture settings, are equally important. Indeed, they are especially important for the kinds of deep learning and rethinking required of students in effectively dealing with controversial issues. Both active learning and a more sophisticated approach to controversial issues make our classes more welcoming to students from diverse backgrounds.[29] The strategies I suggest make teaching more inclusive, more effective, and more fun.

Table 3. Twenty-one questions that underlie the "Big-Burger" model.

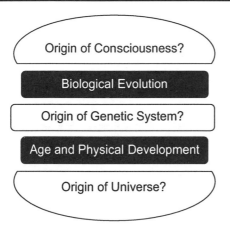

In the hamburger model the three layers of "bun" are areas where there are currently no solid scientific answers, only somewhat-informed, somewhat-airy speculation.

For the most part, the Gradual Creation position (see Table 2 for further detail) matches that of the non-theistic (Basic Science) position, except in the three bun areas, where it goes beyond science to assert the actions of a Creator.

The two layers of "meat" are areas where science has comparatively solid answers. The comparisons on the pages that follow in the sections symbolized by the two layers of meat show that large-scale physical change and macroevolution have occurred—that is, they are strongly inferred facts ("the planets orbit the Sun" is a strongly inferred fact). The headings "lines of evidence" and "applications" provide only brief illustrative examples of the basic science position.

Table 3. continued

Top Layer of Bun: The Origin of Consciousness

Question 1. How does consciousness arise out of molecular and cellular processes?

- **Quick Creation**: Consciousness is a consequence of souls.
- **Gradual Creation**: God individually implants souls, and this act underlies differences in (moral) consciousness between humans and animals.
- **Basic Science**: Consciousness evolved; it is present in apes and, though less well developed, in some other animals. But the mechanisms for evolution of consciousness are not at all clear, leading to much somewhat-informed speculation.
  - ♦ *Lines of evidence*: Observations show that apes are able to recognize themselves in mirrors, recognize paint on their faces, and actively deceive each other and humans. (See also question 14 of the table, p. 51.) Souls are not amenable to scientific analysis (no fossil record, etc.), so science can neither confirm nor disprove their existence or origin.

Top Layer of Meat: Biological Evolution

Group A: Classification and Geographic Distribution

Question 2. Why do related species and genera usually occur in geographically adjacent areas?

- **Quick Creation**: Offers no explanation other than God chose to create this pattern. This does not answer the question, as the same explanation would be given if, for example, structurally similar species were always widely separated geographically.
- **Basic Science**: Related species evolved from common ancestors and have not widely dispersed.
  - ♦ *Lines of evidence*: Existing patterns of species distribution: relationships are confirmed by both functional DNA sequences and non-functional pseudogenes.
  - ♦ *Applications*: We look in adjacent geographical areas for related groups to find additional compounds and genes of medical or agricultural interest.

Question 3. Why is diversity "Linnaean"? (Why do we find discrete, nested groups?)

- **Quick Creation:** Offers no explanation other than God chose to create this pattern. This does not answer the question, as the same explanation would be given if the groups formed a spectrum (or some other pattern) instead of a nested hierarchy.
- **Basic Science:** Each group's core similarities are inherited from a common ancestor by transmission of DNA. More inclusive groups (mammals are more inclusive than primates and rodents) had earlier common ancestors (the common ancestor of all mammals lived earlier in time than the common ancestor of all primates or the common ancestor of all rodents).

Table 3. continued

- ◆ *Lines of evidence*: Linnaeus' initial evidence for this pattern was morphological (physical) similarity. Strong confirmation of these patterns comes from molecular sequences and fossil groups.
- ◆ *Applications*: We look in related groups for related compounds and genes of medical or agricultural interest.
- ◆ *Darwin as "Newton" of biology*: The pattern was clearly delineated by Linnaeus but not explained until Darwin. This relationship parallels Newton's explanation of Copernicus' patterns of planetary motion (see text).

Group B: Fossil Record

Question 4. Why do new groups in the fossil record originate in geographical areas where biologically related groups occurred previously?

- **Quick Creation:** Offers no explanation other than God chose to create this pattern. This does not answer the question, as the same explanation would be given if structurally similar but more recent species were always widely separated geographically from earlier forms in the same taxonomic group.
- **Basic Science:** The new groups had to evolve from biologically appropriate ancestors—those that carried the genes that underlie the structurally similar characters.
  - ◆ *Lines of evidence*: There are many cases of these patterns from the fossil record. Rhinoceros-sized marsupial wombats and giant kangaroos (also marsupials) occurred in Australia—where marsupials occur earlier in the fossil record—at the same time that giant placental mammals were found on other continents. Darwin correctly predicted that ape-human fossil links would be found in Africa. Many geographic regularities, for both living and fossil groups, are the results of plate tectonics moving pieces of continents and carrying the animals and plants along. This pattern allows us to predict the geological formations and geographic areas where new fossil links (older links between apes and humans, for example) are likely to be found.

Question 5. How much change should we find in the fossil record?

- **Quick Creation:** None, or just extinction. Proposes that an illusion of change may occur as a result of mobility and hydrodynamic sorting during the flood. These proposals don't explain the sequences (the evidence) for reefs, plants, etc.
- **Basic Science:** Immense change is expected because the complexity and diversity we see today had to evolve. Well before any early fossils were known, Darwin predicted that life started with a few very simple life forms.
  - ◆ *Lines of evidence*: The fossil record shows that only bacteria existed for the first 1.5 (out of 3.8) billion years. No land plants or land animals are found until the most recent 10% of the fossil record, and all *Homo* are found in the most recent 0.1%. (See Skehan's article, p. 19, for an illustration.)

Table 3. continued

♦ *Comment:* Darwin had no fossil support for evolution, but the fossil record provided a major test and after-the-fact confirmation of his theory.
♦ *Applications:* The stratigraphic sequences for some fossils are important when looking for oil.

Question 6. Why has evolutionary change taken so long?
- **Quick Creation:** No explanation is offered, as no evolutionary change is recognized, and the bulk of the fossil record is explained as having been formed in a year-long flood.
- **Basic Science:** Initial oxygen concentrations on Earth were very low; therefore organisms more complex than bacteria (i.e., eukaryotes) had to wait on free atmospheric oxygen before they could diversify. Land animals and plants could only evolve much later, after higher oxygen levels allowed an effective ozone shield to form, blocking out most of the ultraviolet radiation.
  ♦ *Lines of evidence:* The extent to which minerals were oxidized (as in ferric versus ferrous iron) at different geological times provides a record of the extent to which oxygen was available. Geological processes (plate tectonics) control oxygen levels by controlling the rate of photosynthesis (by changing the area of shallow seas) and the rates at which oxygen is used up by newly-exposed sediments and unweathered rocks.

Question 7. Why do we find fossils that are transitional between major groups?
- **Quick Creation:** Explicitly predicts that no transitions have ever existed, so none can be found.
- **Basic Science:** Major transitions must have existed if organisms formed through evolution. Because evolutionary change is slow, many of the transitions could be retained in the fossil record.
  ♦ *Lines of evidence:* We have found fossils linking invertebrates to fish, fish to amphibians, amphibians to reptiles, and reptiles to birds and mammals. As Darwin predicted, a number of fossils linking apes and humans together have been found in Africa.

Question 8. Why do most fossils occur in ecologically sensible assemblages?
- **Quick Creation:** No explanation is offered, as ecologically sensible communities would have been shuffled by the flood.
- **Basic Science:** Most fossils were buried in or near the communities in which they lived.
  ♦ *Lines of evidence:* Most deposits contain fossils from only one or a few communities. This is especially true for the best-preserved sets of fossils. This, like much of the physical geology of the deposits, rules out a global flood as the major source of sediments.

Table 3. continued

Group C: Evolutionary Processes

Question 9. How have many structural aspects of organisms become adapted (well matched) to their functions?
- **Quick Creation:** The species were individually designed by a Creator.
- **Basic Science:** Natural selection: Organisms whose characteristics allowed them to survive and reproduce better left more descendents. Thus, structures generally became better matched to functions.
  - ◆ *Lines of evidence:* Natural selection has been verified by artificial selection and observation of wild populations.
  - ◆ *Applications:* Artificial selection is used when developing new crops and is important in understanding development of crop resistance to pesticides and disease resistance to antibiotics and other medicines.
  - ◆ *Darwin as "Newton" of biology*: The pattern of widespread adaptation was clearly summarized by Paley but not explained until Darwin. This parallels Newton's explanation of Copernicus' planetary patterns.

Question 10. Why are so many aspects of organismal structure simultaneously both not adaptive and similar to those found in related groups?
- **Quick Creation:** No explanation is offered, as this contradicts direct design. Some suggest degeneration following ejection from Eden, but that does not explain why the degenerate characteristics would resemble characteristics found in related groups.
- **Basic Science:** In many cases these aspects are inherited from ancestors. Every feature of every creature reflects its evolutionary history as well as adaptation.
  - ◆ *Lines of evidence:* Many aspects of structure and physiology reflect ancestry rather than adaptation. Vestigial characteristics provide one set of examples—in humans these include wisdom teeth, the cavity in the appendix, and ear-wagging muscles. Characteristics that develop in embryos but disappear before organisms are born or hatched provide another set (e.g., some human embryonic gill arches or fetal teeth in baleen whales). A third set encompasses characteristics that are adaptive, but whose form is strange or inefficient in ways that reflect ancestry. The nerve to the larynx in the mammalian throat passes down the neck, around the aorta, and back up the neck to the larynx—an especially indirect route in giraffes.
  - ◆ *Comment:* Darwin summarized these examples as "whole great classes of facts" that his theory explained.
  - ◆ *Applications:* This is the core of the new field of Darwinian medicine (see references in text).

Question 11. How do new species form?
- **Quick Creation:** They don't, or are only variants within created "kinds." Each kind was created separately.

Table 3. continued

- **Basic Science:** New species form through several processes, including geographic isolation or changes in the number of sets of chromosomes (polyploidy).
  - ◆ *Lines of evidence:* By experimentally making particular polyploids, we can remake existing species of plants and make new ones that are fully isolated from their still-living ancestors. The more extreme breeds of dogs (e.g., Chihuahua and Great Dane) cannot interbreed successfully. Thus, they would be separate species if the other breeds and mixed-breed dogs didn't exist.
  - ◆ *Applications:* Human-made plant species are commercially important and are found in many flower gardens (e.g., large-flowered petunias).

Question 12. How does life, once started, become structurally more complex?

- **Quick Creation**: It doesn't—only micro-evolutionary change (within kind) is possible, and this cannot produce major new levels of structural complexity.
- **Basic Science:** Major increases in structural complexity occur by symbiosis and gene duplication followed by selective differentiation of the copies to perform different functions. (For example, the sequences of myoglobin and the various hemoglobins were derived by duplication from a single ancestral gene.)
  - ◆ *Lines of evidence:* DNA sequences demonstrate extensive and sequential duplication of genes. Further, DNA sequences of mitochondria and chloroplasts are clearly bacterial, and thus these organelles are symbiotic in origin. Some molecular sequences suggest that even the deepest surviving lineages were mosaics, combining genes of different origins. Moreover, symbiotic root fungi are key to the ability of plants to thrive in upland habitats; and bacterial and protozoa in animals' digestive systems are key to their ability to digest plants.

Question 13. How do new or exceptionally complex characteristics form?

- **Quick Creation:** Unique and complex characteristics are taken as evidence of design and, lacking evolution, can only have been formed by a Creator. This argument is based fundamentally on an assertion that there is no reasonable way for these characteristics to evolve, and thus collapses if a reasonable way is found.
- **Basic Science:** New, complex characteristics can evolve in at least two ways. First, natural section can produce a fairly gradual improvement of a function such as vision. For example, the simplest known photoreceptors are simple pigment spots. Structural complexity increases sequentially through eyes that are simple cups, to eyes that are jelly-filled cups to image-forming eyes. The second major way is by a change in function followed by gradual improvement for the new function. Fossils suggest, for example, that insect wings first served as larval gills for breathing at the surface of the water, allowing them to evolve gradually to a reasonable size. They could then be expressed in adult insects

Table 3. continued

and used for propulsion, first for skittering across the surface of the water, and then, following gradual improvement for faster skittering, for flight.

♦ *Lines of evidence:* Gradual improvement: series of existing or fossil organs such as eyes. Change in function: similarities in core structure (forearms, wings, and paddles in vertebrates) or in embryology (two mammalian middle ear bones start as part of the nascent jaw in the fetuses).

Question 14. Has culture developed from animal antecedents?
- **Quick Creation:** No.
- **Basic Science:** Yes, it too evolved.
  ♦ *Lines of evidence:* In the wild, apes (and some monkeys) use tools spontaneously. Some wild apes make simple tools and some carefully teach their young to use them as well. Anthropologists define making and using tools and teaching others to use them as core aspects of culture.

Middle Layer of Bun: Origin of Genetic System?

Question 15. Origin of genetic system? (Specifically, how did a genetic system mediated by transfer-RNA get started)?
- **Quick Creation:** Divine intervention.
- **Gradual Creation:** Divine intervention or natural processes.
- **Basic Science:** Natural processes.
  ♦ *Lines of evidence:* There is very little direct evidence for how the genetic system first formed.
  ♦ *Comment:* Once the universe starts in a Big Bang, its development at least up through the origin of planets and the syntheses of diverse organic molecules is inevitable, given the basic processes of physics and chemistry (see question 16, below). The probability of developing a genetic code is unknown. Once the code is working, genetics and natural selection make evolution a physical necessity. However, many specific details of evolutionary history, such as whether the land could have been inhabited, appear to depend on particular geological circumstances that allowed an ozone shield.

Lower Layer of Meat: Age and Physical Development

Question 16. What was the origin of organic molecules and simple systems prior to life with genetic code?
- **Quick Creation:** Life began within days of the origin of the universe, precluding any lengthy period of earlier synthesis.
- **Basic Science:** They were synthesized by natural chemical processes.
  ♦ *Lines of evidence:* Basic organic chemistry shows that organic molecules must form in a hydrogen-rich environment, and the universe is about 98% hydrogen. Experiments verify that some organic molecules MUST form in virtually any non-oxidizing environment. Further, organic molecules are found within some meteorites and are routinely detected in interplanetary space by radio-telescopes.

Table 3. continued

♦ *Applications:* Organic syntheses that are the same or similar to those that form interstellar molecules are also very important in industrial chemistry.

Question 17. Over how long a period did the geological record form?
- **Quick Creation:** Quickly, in a year-long flood.
- **Basic Science:** Slowly, by gradual processes and local catastrophes.
  - ♦ *Lines of evidence:* Most fossils occur in ecologically sensible local assemblages. Most physical features of sedimentary rocks are incompatible with a global flood. Examples include thousands of meters of limestone formed from oceanic ooze, ancient lake beds with millions of varves (annual layers), and fossilized reefs with the coral heads pointed to the position of the ancient Sun, as reconstructed from paleomagnetic evidence of continental drift. This is all in addition to the various techniques for estimating the ages of deposits.
  - ♦ *Applications:* Starting in the 1960s, plate tectonics revolutionized geological explanation and allowed us for the first time to understand the distributions of earthquakes and volcanoes—the processes by which mountains have formed—and the structural features of Earth's crust in general. These same ideas now underlie oil exploration and the explanations for where we find economically valuable minerals, as well as major features of both current and ancient animal distributions.

Question 18. How old are the universe and Earth?
- **Quick Creation:** 8,000 to 20,000 years, as estimated from Biblical genealogies and narratives.
- **Basic Science:** Billions of years.
  - ♦ *Lines of evidence:* The immense age of Earth was first evident from analyses of rates of erosion and deposition. Immense age is now explicit in fundamental geological explanations, including plate tectonics (time for continents to move and for mountains to form) and in the results of radioactive dating (which could have shown that no rocks were older than 20,000 years but instead showed that the oldest are about 4 billion years old on Earth and 4.65 billion years old on the moon and in meteorites). Astronomy also requires an old age to explain the development of stellar clusters, the oldest of which would have required more than 10 billion years to reach their current state. Finally, an old age is required to account for how far out we can see into the depths of space. Because light takes time to travel, to see into space is to look into the past. (If the universe were only 20,000 years old we should only be able to see 20,000 light years away. But the Milky Way alone is 100,000 light years across, and we can see some 10 billion light years away and, therefore, some 10 billion years into the past.)
  - ♦ *Applications:* Great age is fundamental to most of geology and astronomy and is implicit in the match of many features of the universe with nuclear

Table 3. continued

physics (quantum mechanics) and relativity. Age coupled with plate tectonics is now powerful in geological explanation and mineral exploration. Quantum mechanics is important in electronics, computers, nuclear reactors, and nuclear medicine.

Question 19. What is the magnitude of physical change of the universe since its initial days?

- **Quick Creation:** By the end of Creation week the Earth was covered with all of the kinds of living organisms. There has been some physical and biological degeneration since the fall, but only enough to account for the changes from Eden to now.
- **Basic Science:** The universe apparently started out so hot and dense that no atoms or elements could exist. Expansion cooled the universe and made it less dense. Initial element formation led almost exclusively to hydrogen and helium. (The oldest stars are nearly pure hydrogen and helium.) The other elements were synthesized in these simple stars or when the stars exploded. The elements were then dispersed throughout their galaxies when the stars exploded. This dispersion allowed the subsequent formation of stars that had planets and the syntheses of organic molecules.
    - ♦ *Lines of evidence:* Red-shift increases with distance (Hubble's Law), showing that the universe is expanding. The cosmic microwave background appears to be the fireball from the Big Bang cooled by this expansion to three degrees absolute. The oldest stars lack metals and so could have had neither planets nor life.
    - ♦ *Applications:* Relativity and quantum mechanics govern these changes. Quantum mechanics is important in electronics, computers, nuclear reactors, and nuclear medicine.

Question 20. Direction of change of thermodynamic order in the universe?

- **Quick Creation:** Decrease in order after Eden.
- **Basic Science:** The second law of thermodynamics requires a system-level decrease in thermodynamic order (i.e., from very hot particles everywhere to mostly space with scant low temperature radiation). Can increase order in subsystems by input of energy from other parts.
    - ♦ *Lines of evidence:* Second law of thermodynamics.
    - ♦ *Applications:* Second law is fundamental to physics and, thus, engineering.

Lower Layer of Bun: Origin of Universe?

Question 21. What is the origin of the universe?

- **Quick Creation:** Created—Creation week.
- **Gradual Creation:** Created—Big Bang or "inflation."
- **Basic Science:** We have mainly some highly speculative scientific ideas on origins and start of Big Bang (or of inflation).

Notes

[1] For recent summaries see especially: BSCS 1993, Bransford et al. 1999, Boyer Commission 1998, Feldman and Paulsen 1998, NRC 1996, NSF 1996, Pescosolido and Aminzade 1999, Uno 1999, Walvoord and Anderson 1998. For longer presentations of many of the points I make here see Nelson 1986, Nelson et al. 1998, Nickels et al. 1996.

[2] 1998.

[3] 1997.

[4] 1993.

[5] Treisman and Fullilove 1990.

[6] For example, Larson 1992, Nelson 1999.

[7] Flammer et al. 1999.

[8] Nelson 1989, 1994, 1997, 1999.

[9] AAAS 1989, 1993; NSF, 1996.

[10] Strahler 1999.

[11] 1859.

[12] Glen 1982, Strahler 1999.

[13] 1978.

[14] Strahler 1999.

[15] Glen 1982.

[16] Freeman and Herron 1998

[17] Ness and Williams 1996, Trevathan et al. 1999.

[18] Hawking 1998.

[19] 1998, 1999.

[20] Nelson 1986.

[21] 1982.

[22] Matsumura 1995.

[23] For example, Lawson 1992, Perry 1970, Nelson 1999.

[24] Belenkey et al. 1986, King and Kitchner 1994, Nelson 1999.

[25] For example, de Waal 1997

[26] 1987, 1998.

[27] 1999.

[28] 1999.

[29] Nelson 1996.

References

American Association for the Advancement of Science (AAAS). 1989. *Science for All Americans*. Washington, DC: AAAS Publications.

———— 1993. *Benchmarks for Scientific Literacy*. New York: Oxford University Press.

Angelo, T.A., and K.P. Cross. 1993. *Classroom Assessment Techniques,* 2nd ed. San Francisco: Jossey-Bass.

Augustine of Hippo, St.. 401–415 AD. *De Genesi ad litteram libri duodecim* (The Literal Meaning of Genesis). Translated by John Hammond Taylor, 1982 volume 41 in *Ancient Christian Writers: the Works of the Fathers in Translation*. New York: Newman Press.

Belenky, M.F., B.M. Clinchy, N.R. Goldberger, and J.R. Tarule. 1986. *Women's Ways of Knowing*. New York: Basic Books.

Biological Sciences Curriculum Study. 1993. *Developing Biological Literacy*. Colorado Springs, BSCS.

Boyer Commission on Educating Undergraduates in the Research University. 1998. *Reinventing Undergraduate Education: A Blueprint for America's Research Universities*. New York: Carnegie Foundation for the Advancement of Teaching. Text available online at: http://notes.cc.sunysb.edu/Pres/boyer.nsf

Bransford, J.D., A.L. Brown, and R.R. Cocking, eds. 1999. *How People Learn: Brain, Mind, Experience, and School*. Washington, DC: National Academy Press.

Bronowski, J. 1978. *The Origins of Knowledge and Imagination*. New Haven: Yale University Press.

Darwin, C. 1859. *On the Origin of Species*. London: John Murray.

de Waal, F. 1997. *Good Natured: The Origins of Right and Wrong in Humans and Other Animals*. Cambridge, MA: Harvard University Press.

Feldman, K.A., and M.B. Paulsen, eds. 1998. *Teaching and Learning in the College Classroom*, second edition. Ginn Press.

Flammer, L. et al. 1999. Evolution and the Nature of Science Institutes. *www.indiana.edu/~ensiweb*.

Glen, W. 1982. *The Road to Jaramillo: Critical Years of the Revolution in Earth Science*. Stanford, CA: Stanford University Press.

Hake, R.R. 1998. Interactive-engagement vs traditional methods: A six-thousand-student survey of mechanics test data for introductory physics courses. *American Journal of Physics,* 66, 64–74. Text available online at: http://carini.physics.indiana.edu/SDI/welcome.html#z44.

Hawking, S. 1998. *A Brief History of Time*, 10th anniversary ed. New York: Bantam Doubleday Dell.

King, P.M., and K.S. Kitchner. 1994. *Developing Reflexive Judgment: Understanding and Promoting Intellectual Growth and Critical Thinking in Adolescents and Adults*. San Francisco: Jossey-Bass.

Kitcher, P. 1982. *Abusing Science*. Cambridge, MA: M.I.T. Press.

Larson, A.A., and W.A. Worsnop. 1992. Learning about evolution and rejecting a belief in Special Creation: Effects of reflective reasoning skill, prior knowledge, prior belief, and religious commitment. *Journal of Research in Science Teaching,* 29(2):143–166.

Matsumura, M. 1995. *Voices for Evolution*. Berkeley, CA: The National Center for Science Education.

National Academy of Sciences (NAS) 1998. *Teaching About Evolution and the Nature of Science*. Washington, DC: National Academy Press. Text available online at: http://books.nap.edu/html/evolution98/.

———— 1999. *Science and Creationism: A View from the National Academy of Sciences*. Second edition. Washington, DC: National Academy Press. Text available online at: http://books.nap.edu/html/creationism/.

National Research Council (NRC). 1990. *Fulfilling the Promise: Biology Education in the Nation's Schools*. Washington, DC: National Academy Press.

———— 1996. *National Science Education Standards*. Washington, DC, National Academy Press. Text available online at: http://books.nap.edu/html/nses/.

———— 1999. *Transforming Undergraduate Education in Science, Mathematics, Engineering, and Technology*. Washington, DC: National Academy Press. Text available online at: http://books.nap.edu/catalog/6453.html.

National Science Foundation (NSF), Division of Undergraduate Education. 1996. *Shaping the Future: New Expectations for Undergraduate Education in Science, Mathematics, Engineering, and Technology.* Washington, DC: NSF. Text available online at: http://www.ehr.nsf.gov/ehr/due/documents/review/96139/start.htm.

Nelson, C.E. 1986. Creation, evolution, or both? A multiple model approach. In *Science and Creation*, edited by R.W. Hanson. New York: Macmillan.

Nelson, C.E. 1989. Skewered on the unicorn's horn: The illusion of [a] tragic tradeoff between content and critical thinking in the teaching of science. In *Enhancing Critical Thinking in the Sciences*, edited by L. Crow. Washington, DC: Society for College Science Teachers.

Nelson, C.E. 1994. Critical thinking and collaborative learning. In *Collaborative Learning and College Teaching*, edited by K. Bosworth and S. Hamilton. San Francisco: Jossey-Bass.

Nelson, C.E. 1996. Student diversity requires different approaches to college teaching, even in math and science. *American Behavioral Scientist* 40:165–175.

Nelson, C.E. 1997. Tools for tampering with teaching's taboos. In *New Paradigms for College Teaching*, edited by W.E. Campbell and K.A. Smith. Edina, MN: Interaction Book Company.

Nelson, C.E. 1999. On the persistence of unicorns: the tradeoff between content and critical thinking revisited. In *The Social Worlds of Higher Education: Handbook for Teaching in a New Century*, edited by B.A. Pescosolido and R. Aminzade. Thousand Oaks, CA: Pine Forge Press.

Nelson, C.E., M.K. Nickels, and J. Beard. 1998. The nature of science as a foundation for teaching science: evolution as a case study. In *The Nature of Science in Science Education*, edited by W.F. McComas. Boston: Kluwer Academic Publishers.

Nesse, R.M., and G.C. Williams. 1996. *Why We Get Sick: The New Science of Darwinian Medicine*. New York: Random House.

Nickels, M. 1987. Human evolution: a challenge for biology teachers. *The American Biology Teacher*, 49(3):143–148.

Nickels, M. 1998. Humans as a case study for the evidence of evolution. *Reports of the National Center for Science Education* 18(5):24–27.

Nickels, M., C.E. Nelson, and J. Beard. 1996. Better biology teaching by emphasizing evolution and the nature of science. *The American Biology Teacher* 58(6):332-336.

Overton, Judge William R. 1982. *McLean v. Arkansas Board of Education*, decision. U.S. District Court. 529 F. Supp. 1255 (E.D. AK)

Pennock, R.T. 1999. *Tower of Babel: The Evidence Against the New Creationism*. Cambridge, MA: M.I.T. Press.

Perry, W.G., Jr. 1970. *Forms of Intellectual and Ethical Development in the College Years: A Scheme*. New York: Holt, Rinehart and Winston.

Pescosolido, B.A., and R. Aminzade, eds. 1999. *The Social Worlds of Higher Education: Handbook for Teaching in a New Century*. Thousand Oaks, CA: Pine Forge Press. With a companion CD: J.H. Shin et al. 1999. *Field Guide for Teaching in a New Century: Ideas from Fellow Travelers*.

Skehan S.J., J.W. 2000. Modern science and the book of Genesis. In *The Creation Controversy & The Science Classroom*. Arlington, VA: National Science Teachers Association.

Springer, L., M. Stanne, and S. Donovan. 1997. Effects of Small-Group Learning on Undergraduates in Science, Mathematics, Engineering, and Technology: A Meta-Analysis. Research Monograph No. 11. National Institute for Science Education, University of Wisconsin–Madison.

Strahler, A.N. 1999. *Science and Earth History: The Evolution/Creation Controversy,* 2nd printing with new preface. Buffalo, NY: Prometheus Books.

Treisman, U., and R.E. Fullilove. 1990. Mathematics achievement among African American undergraduates at the University of California, Berkeley: an evaluation of the mathematics workshop program. Journal of Negro Education 59:463–478.

Trevathan, W., J.J. McKenna, and E.O. Smith, eds. 1999. *Evolutionary Medicine*. Oxford, England: Oxford University Press.

Uno, G.E. 1999. *Handbook on Teaching Undergraduate Science Courses: A Survival Training Manual*. Fort Worth, TX: Harcourt College Publishers.

Walvoord, B.E.F., and V.J. Anderson. 1998. *Effective Grading: A Tool for Learning and Assessment*. San Francisco: Jossey-Bass.

An NSTA Position Statement

The Teaching of Evolution

Adopted by the NSTA Board of Directors in July 1997

Introductory Remarks

The National Science Teachers Association supports the position that evolution is a major unifying concept of science and should be included as part of K–college science frameworks and curricula. NSTA recognizes that evolution has not been emphasized in science curricula in a manner commensurate to its importance because of official policies, intimidation of science teachers, the general public's misunderstanding of evolutionary theory, and a century of controversy.

Furthermore, teachers are being pressured to introduce creationism, creation "science," and other nonscientific views, which are intended to weaken or eliminate the teaching of evolution.

Within this context, NSTA recommends that:

- Science curricula and teachers should emphasize evolution in a manner commensurate with its importance as a unifying concept in science and its overall explanatory power.

- Policy makers and administrators should not mandate policies requiring the teaching of creation science or related concepts such as so-called "intelligent design," "abrupt appearance," and "arguments against evolution."

- Science teachers should not advocate any religious view about creation, nor advocate the converse: that there is no possibility of supernatural influence in bringing about the universe as we know it. Teachers should be nonjudgmental about the personal beliefs of students.

- Administrators should provide support to teachers as they design and implement curricula that emphasize evolution. This should include inservice education to assist teachers to teach evolution in a comprehensive and professional manner. Administrators also should support teachers against pressure to promote nonscientific views or to diminish or eliminate the study of evolution.

- Parental and community involvement in establishing the goals of science education and the curriculum development process should be encouraged and nurtured in our democratic society. However, the professional responsibility of science teachers and curriculum specialists to provide students with quality science education should not be bound by censorship, pseudoscience, inconsistencies, faulty scholarship, or unconstitutional mandates.

- Science textbooks shall emphasize evolution as a unifying concept. Publishers should not be required or volunteer to include disclaimers in textbooks concerning the nature and study of evolution.

NSTA offers the following background information:

The Nature of Science and Scientific Theories

Science is a method of explaining the natural world. It assumes the universe operates according to regularities and that through systematic investigation we can understand these regularities. The methodology of science emphasizes the logical testing of alternate explanations of natural phenomena against empirical data. Because science is limited to explaining the natural world by means of natural processes, it cannot use supernatural causation in its explanations. Similarly, science is precluded from making statements about supernatural forces, because these are outside its provenance. Science has increased our knowledge because of this insistence on the search for natural causes.

The most important scientific explanations are called "theories." In ordinary speech, "theory" is often used to mean "guess," or "hunch," whereas in scientific terminology, a theory is a set of universal statements that explain the natural world. Theories are powerful tools. Scientists seek to develop theories that

- are internally consistent and compatible with the evidence

- are firmly grounded in and based upon evidence

- have been tested against a diverse range of phenomena

- possess broad and demonstrable effectiveness in problem-solving

- explain a wide variety of phenomena.

The body of scientific knowledge changes as new observations and discoveries are made. Theories and other explanations change. New theories emerge and other theories are modified or discarded. Throughout this process, theories are formulated and tested on the basis of evidence, internal consistency, and their explanatory power.

Evolution as a Unifying Concept

Evolution in the broadest sense can be defined as the idea that the universe has a history: that change through time has taken place. If we look today at the galaxies, stars, the planet Earth, and the life on planet Earth, we see that things today are different from what they were in the past: galaxies, stars, planets, and life forms have evolved. Biological evolution refers to the scientific theory that living things share ancestors from which they have diverged: Darwin called it "descent with modification." There is abundant and consistent evidence from astronomy, physics, biochemistry, geochronology, geology, biology, anthropology, and other sciences that evolution has taken place.

As such, evolution is a unifying concept for science. The *National Science Education Standards* recognizes that conceptual schemes such as evolution "unify science disciplines and provide students with powerful ideas to help them understand the natural world," and recommends evolution as one such scheme. In addition, the *Benchmarks for Science Literacy* from the American Association for the Advancement of Science's Project 2061, and NSTA's *Scope, Sequence, and Coordination Project*, as well as other national calls for science reform, all name evolution as a unifying concept because of its importance across the discipline of science. Scientific disciplines with a historical component, such as astronomy, geology, biology, and anthropology, cannot be taught with integrity if evolution is not emphasized.

There is no longer a debate among scientists over whether evolution has taken place. There is considerable debate about how evolution has taken place: the processes and mechanisms producing change, and what has happened during the history of the universe. Scientists often disagree about their explanations. In any science, disagreements are subject to rules of evaluation. Errors and false conclusions are confronted by experiment and observation, and evolution, as in any aspect of science, is continually open to and subject to experimentation and questioning.

Creationism

The word "creationism" has many meanings. In its broadest meaning, creationism is the idea that a supernatural power or powers created. Thus to Christians, Jews, and Muslims, God created; to the Navajo, the Hero Twins created. In a narrower sense, "creationism" has come to mean "special creation": the doctrine that the universe and all that is in it was created by God in essentially its present form, at one time. The most common variety of special creationism asserts that

- the Earth is very young

- life was originated by a creator

- life appeared suddenly

- kinds of organisms have not changed

- all life was designed for certain functions and purposes

This version of special creation is derived from a literal interpretation of Biblical Genesis. It is a specific, sectarian religious belief that is not held by all religious people. Many Christians and Jews believe that God created through the process of evolution. Pope John Paul II, for example, issued a statement in 1996 that reiterated the Catholic position that God created, but that the scientific evidence for evolution is strong.

"Creation science" is an effort to support special creationism through methods of science. Teachers are often pressured to include it or synonyms such as "intelligent design theory," "abrupt appearance theory," "initial complexity theory," or "arguments against evolution" when they teach evolution. Special creationist claims have been discredited by the available evidence. They have no power to explain the natural world and its diverse phenomena. Instead, creationists seek out supposed anomalies among many existing theories and accepted facts. Furthermore, creation science claims do not provide a basis for solving old or new problems or for acquiring new information.

Nevertheless, as noted in the *National Science Education Standards,* "Explanations on how the natural world changed based on myths, personal beliefs, religious values, mystical inspiration, superstition, or authority may be personally useful and socially relevant, but they are not scientific." Because science can only use natural explanations and not supernatural ones, science teachers should not advocate any religious view about creation, nor advocate the converse: that there is no possibility of supernatural influence in bringing about the universe as we know it.

Legal Issues

Several judicial rulings have clarified issues surrounding the teaching of evolution and the imposition of mandates that creation science be taught when evolution is taught. The First Amendment of the Constitution requires that public institutions such as schools be religiously neutral; because special creation is a specific, sectarian religious view, it cannot be advocated as "true," accurate scholarship in the public schools. When Arkansas passed a law requiring "equal time" for creationism and evolution, the law was challenged in Federal District Court. Opponents of the bill included the religious leaders of the United Methodist, Episcopalian, Roman Catholic, African Methodist Episcopal, Presbyterian, and Southern Baptist churches, and several educational organizations. After a full trial, the judge ruled that creation science did not qualify as a scientific theory (*McLean v. Arkansas Board of Education*, 529 F. Supp. 1255 (ED Ark. 1982)).

Louisiana's equal time law was challenged in court, and eventually reached the Supreme Court. In *Edwards v. Aguillard*, 482 U.S. 578 (1987), the court determined that creationism was inherently a religious idea, and to mandate or advocate it in the public schools would be unconstitutional. Other court decisions have upheld the right of a district to require that a teacher teach evolution and not to teach creation science (*Webster v. New Lennox School District* #122, 917 F.2d 1003 (7th Cir. 1990); *Peloza v. Capistrano Unified School District*, 37 F.3d 517 (9th Cir. 1994)).

Some legislatures and policy makers continue attempts to distort the teaching of evolution through mandates that would require teachers to teach evolution as "only a theory," or that require a textbook or lesson on evolution to be preceded by a disclaimer. Regardless of the legal status of these mandates, they are bad educational policy. Such policies have the effect of intimidating teachers, which may result in the de-emphasis or omission of evolution. The public will only be further confused about the special nature of scientific theories, and if less evolution is learned by students, science literacy itself will suffer.

References

Aldridge, B.G., ed. 1996. *Scope, Sequence, and Coordination: A High School Framework for Science Education*. Arlington, VA: National Science Teachers Association.

American Association for the Advancement of Science, Project 2061. 1993. *Benchmarks for Science Literacy*. New York: Oxford University Press.

Daniel v. Waters, 515 F.2d 485 (6th Cir. 1975).

Edwards v. Aguillard, 482 U.S. 578 (1987).

Epperson v. Arkansas, 393 U.S. 97 (1968).

Laudan, L. 1996. *Beyond Positivism and Relativism: Theory, Method, and Evidence*. Boulder, CO: Westview Press.

McLean v. Arkansas Board of Education, 529 F. Supp. 1255 (ED Ark. 1982).

National Research Council. 1996. *The National Science Education Standards*. Washington, DC: National Academy Press.

National Science Teachers Association NSTA. 1993. *Scope, Sequence, and Coordination of Secondary School Science. Vol. 1. The Content Core: A Guide for Curriculum Designers* (Rev. ed). Arlington, VA: NSTA.

Peloza v. Capistrano Unified School District, 37 F.3d 517 (9th Cir. 1994).

Ruse, Michael. 1996. *But Is It Science?: The Philosophical Question in the Creation/Evolution Controversy*. Amherst, NY: Prometheus.

Webster v. New Lennox School District #122, 917 F.2d 1003 (7th Cir. 1990).

Recommended Readings

These resources are intended as a list of recommendations beyond what is already listed in the References sections of the articles in *The Creation Controversy & The Science Classroom*.

Dalrymple, G. Brent. 1994. *The Age of the Earth*. Stanford, CA: Stanford University Press.

Dennett, D. 1995. *Darwin's Dangerous Idea*. New York: Simon and Schuster.

Futuyama, D.J. 1995. *Science on Trial: The Case for Evolution*. Sunderland, MA: Sinauer Press.

Gilkey, L. 1985. *Creationism on Trial: Evolution and God at Little Rock*. San Francisco: Harper and Row Publishers.

Hanson, R.W. ed. 1986. *Science and Creation*. New York: Macmillan.

Kitcher, P. 1982. *Abusing Science*. Cambridge, MA: M.I.T. Press.

Matsumura, M. ed. 1995. *Voices for Evolution*. Berkeley, CA: The National Center for Science Education.

Mayr, E. 1997. *This Is Biology*. Cambridge, MA: The Belknap Press of Harvard University.

McKown, D.B. 1993. *The Mythmaker's Magic: Behind the Illusion of 'Creation Science.'* Buffalo, NY: Prometheus Books.

National Academy of Sciences. 1999. *Science and Creationism: A View from the National Academy of Sciences*. Second edition. Washington, DC, National Academy Press.

———— 1998. *Teaching About Evolution and the Nature of Science*. Washington, DC: National Academy Press.

Numbers, R.L. 1993. *The Creationists: The Evolution of Scientific Creationism*. Berkeley, CA: University of California Press.

Pennock, R.T. 1999. *Tower of Babel: The Evidence Against the New Creationism*. Cambridge, MA: M.I.T. Press.

Press, F., and R. Siever. 1993. *Earth*. New York: W.H. Freeman.

Ruse, M. 1996. *But Is It Science? The Philosophical Question in the Creation/Evolution Controversy*. Buffalo, NY: Prometheus Books.

Strahler, A.N. 1999. *Science and Earth History: The Evolution/Creation Controversy,* second printing with new preface. Buffalo, NY: Prometheus Books.